LIVES
of the
ENGLISH
SAINTS

L I V E S
o f   t h e
E N G L I S H
S A I N T S

by

S. BARING-GOULD

Selected reprints from the author's sixteen-volume
work 'Lives of the Saints.'

Published in 1990 by Llanerch
ISBN 0947992 41 3

CONTENTS

S. ALBAN, M.

(ABOUT A.D. 304.)

[Martyrology of Bede ; those of Hrabanus, Usuardus, Ado, Notker, &c. Roman Martyrology, Gallican, German, Sarum, and York, but Modern Anglican Reformed Kalendar on the 17th, occasioned by a mistake of printer, XXII. having been altered into XVII. Authorities :—Gildas, or rather the author of the *De Excidio Britannicæ*, called Gildas by Bede. This work was supposed by Dr. T. Wright, "Biographia Britannica Literaria," 1842, to have been a forgery by a Saxon priest, who wrote it with the idea of using the writings of a British priest as an argument against the purity of that native church, which the Roman party were bent on upsetting or forcing into Roman obedience. This view has now been abandoned. Gildas belonged to the Roman party in the Celtic Church which strove to stamp out national peculiarities, and it is certainly a genuine treatise. The British retreating before the Saxons would carry with them the tradition of the martyrdom of S. Alban. That S. Alban's memory had not died out appears from the fact of S. Germain, on his visit to Britain, collecting earth stained, or supposed to be stained, with his blood.[1] Venantius Fortunatus, who died in 609, mentions S. Alban in one of his hymns. The story as given by Gildas contains an inaccuracy. He makes the "noble river Thames" flow by Verulam. As Bede tells it, it contains several improbabilities, and presents chronological difficulties ; for whilst the persecution of Diocletian lasted, under which S. Alban is stated

---

[1] Constantius, Vit. Germani I. 25 (A.D. 473, 492).

to have suffered, Britain was first alienated from the Roman empire by
Carausius and Allectus, and was then under Constantius Chlorus. It is
difficult to believe that Constantius would sanction a bloody persecution
in his dominions, but it is not improbable that local persecutions under
severe governors may have broken out. Gildas's *general* statement re-
specting the persecution by Diocletian rests, as is usual with him, upon an
unauthorised transference to the particular case of Britain of the language
used by Eusebius (Lib. viii., c. 2) relating to the persecution in general,
and is conclusively contradicted by Eusebius himself (viii. c. 13), who says
that in Britain Constantius Chlorus "had no share in the hostility raised
against us, but even preserved and protected those pious persons under
him free from harm and calumny, neither did he demolish the churches,
nor devise any mischief against us." Also Sozomen i. 6, and Lactantius,
who also distinctly asserts that Constantius suffered no Christian to be killed,
but adds, in contradiction to Eusebius, that he allowed the churches to be
pulled down. The *individual* case of S. Alban, however, rests upon a
local tradition traceable apparently up to 429, the date of S. Germain's
first visit to Britain ; and perhaps the general assertions of Eusebius and
the others may leave room for it, and for one or two other martyrdoms.
Though Constantius Chlorus may have discouraged persecution himself,
it is by no means improbable that local persecutions may have broken out
under severe and bigoted magistrates. That S. Alban's martyrdom, however, happened in the Diocletian persecution, rests only on the knowledge,
or according to another reading, the guess (conjicimus for cognoscimus)
of the pseudo-Gildas. And the Anglo-Saxon Chronicle, and the Liber
Landavensis, although the latter still attributes it to that persecution, date
it in 286. All that seems certain is, that within one hundred and twenty-
five years after the last persecution, a belief existed at Verulam that a
martyr named Alban lay buried near that town. If the persecution was
that of Diocletian, the date must have been 304, that persecution beginning
with the first edict of Diocletian in March 303, but extending to laymen
only with his fourth edict in 304, and ceasing altogether in Britain upon
his resignation in 305. In a book of the lives of the abbots of S. Alban's
to the time of Eadwar (circ. 970) it is said that among the ruins of ancient
Verulam was found a stone chest containing a book written in characters
only decipherable by an old monk named Unwyn, who found it to contain
the Acts of S. Alban in ancient British. This was translated into Latin in
the 12th cent. by William of S. Alban's, at the request of the abbot Simon
(d. 1188). These pretended Acts, an impudent forgery of William of S.
Alban's, perpetrated with the connivance of his abbot, purport to have
been written by a British Christian in 590, when the Saxons had overrun
the country and established paganism. In the prologue the author says :--
" I have not given my name, lest I should thereby forfeit both my name

S. ALBAN.

and my life." That most worthless of historians, except as a collector of popular ballads and romances, Geoffrey of Monmouth, also mentions S. Alban, but does not tell his story fully. He also names "S. Amphibalus."]

 AINT ALBAN, a pagan, received into his house and sheltered a Christian priest during the persecution of Diocletian, and was so struck by the devotion to God, and blameless life of the man whom he protected, that he placed himself under instruction and became a Christian. A rumour having reached the governor of Verulam, that the priest was hiding in the house of Alban, he sent soldiers to search it. Alban seeing them arrive, hastily cast the long cloak of the priest over his head and shoulders, and presented himself to the soldiers as the man whom they sought.[1] He was immediately bound and brought before the governor. It fell out that the governor was then standing at the altar and was offering sacrifice. When the cloak was removed, which had concealed the face of Alban, and he perceived that the man was not the priest he had ordered to be arrested, his anger flamed hot, and he ordered Alban immediately to sacrifice or to suffer death.

S. Alban steadfastly refused to offer to idols. Then the magistrate asked, "Of what family and race are you?" "How can it concern thee to know of what stock I am?" answered Alban. "If thou desirest to know what is my religion, I will tell thee—I am a Christian, and am bound by Christian obligations."

"I ask thy name, tell it me immediately."

---

[1] The priest, whose name Bede does not give, was afterwards supplied by the fabricator of the spurious Acts with the name of Amphibalus, from the *cloak* which he wore, Amphibalus being the Greek for a cloak. Bede says that the priest did not suffer then, "his time of martyrdom had not yet come." The forger gave him an absurd name, and invented the acts of his martyrdom. Under the name of Amphibalus this priest figures in some martyrologies on June 22nd with S. Alban, or alone on June 25th.

"I am called Alban by my parents," he replied. "And I worship and adore the true and living God, who created all things."

Then the governor said, "If thou wilt enjoy eternal life, delay not to sacrifice to the great gods."

Alban rejoined, "These sacrifices which are offered to devils are of none avail. Hell is the reward of those who offer them."

The governor ordered S. Alban to be scourged, hoping to shake his constancy by pain. But the martyr bore the stripes patiently, and even joyously, for our Lord's sake. When the judge saw that he could not prevail, he ordered Alban to be put to death. On his way to execution, the martyr had to cross a river. "There," says Bede, "he saw a multitude of both sexes, and of every age and rank, assembled to attend the blessed confessor and martyr; and these so crowded the bridge, that he could not pass over that evening. Then S. Alban, urged by an ardent desire to accomplish his martyrdom, drew near to the stream, and the channel was dried up, making a way for him to pass over."[1]

Then the martyr and his escort, followed by an innumerable company of spectators, ascended the hill now occupied by the abbey church bearing his name. It was then a green hill covered with flowers sloping gently down into the pleasant plain. Then his executioner refused to perform his office, and throwing down his sword confessed himself a Christian. Another man was

---

[1] This "river" is a stream, the Ver; it runs between the present church and the site of Verulam. The miracle of drying up the river is an exaggeration. The Ver is nowhere unfordable, and in Midsummer is the merest brook. At the same time that S. Alban dried up the river, says Bede, he miraculously caused a fountain to spring up on the hill of martyrdom. This is probably Holywell, about half way between the abbey and Sopwell nunnery, in a field on the east side of the street called Holywell Hill.

detailed to deal the blow, and both Alban and the executioner who had refused to strike were decapitated together.

On the site of the martyrdom rose a church directly. that peace was restored, which, though it must have fallen into ruins during the Saxon pagan domination, was restored when the Anglo-Saxons were converted, and stood in the days of Bede. Afterwards, in 793, Offa, king of the Mercians, founded there the stately abbey of S. Alban's. At the time of the Danish invasions, the monks of S. Alban's sent the body of the saint for safety to Ely, and when all fear of the Danes was over, re-claimed the body, but the monks of Ely refused to surrender it, whereupon they of S. Alban's declared that they had never sent the true body of the saint to Ely, but another one; and that the real relics were buried in a secret place at S. Alban's. They proceeded at once to dig them up and enshrine them.[1] The shrines of S. Alban, "S. Amphibalus," and the martyred executioner, have lately been examined, and no traces of the relics were found; they were scattered by the commissioners in the reign of Henry VIII.[2]

The S. Alban venerated this day at Cologne is a different saint, though at Cologne it is pretended that the church of S. Alban in that city contains the relics of the English proto-martyr. The relics of S. Alban at Cologne were brought from Rome in the year 989, and

[1] There can be no manner of doubt that this was a falsehood. The relics scattered at the Reformation in S. Alban's were only those of the second S. Alban. This is not the only indictment against the monks there.

[2] Bede says, writing iu 731, that in the church of S. Alban "to this day the healing of the infirm and the operation of cures does not cease to be famous," although the localities had been forgotten before Offa built his monastery in 793 (Matt. Paris \ it. Off.) Thus, probably enough, the first relics were not genuine. It must be remembered also how scandalous was the forgery of the Acts of S. Alban perpetrated in the same house later.

the supposition that the relics of the proto-martyr of England were carried to Rome after their invention in 793 by King Offa, is destitute of all probability, though it is insisted on by Cologne historians. The S. Alban enshrined at Cologne was given by Pope John XI., to the Empress Theophania, the wife of Otho II., on her visit to Rome in 989; but nothing is known of who this S. Alban was, and how he suffered.

In art S. Alban is represented sometimes in civil, and sometimes in military dress, bearing the palm and sword, or a cross and a sword.

S. Aldhelm (May 25).

S. ALDHELM, B. OF SHERBORNE.

(A.D. 709.)

[Roman and Anglican Martyrologies. His translation on March 31st. Authorities:—A life by William of Malmesbury, written towards the middle of the 12th century; another life written in the latter years of the 11th century, by Faricius, a foreign monk of Malmesbury, who became abbot of Abingdon in 1100, and died in 1117. A copy of the first is preserved in MS., Cotton., Claudius A.v., written in the 12th cent.; fuller copies have been printed by Wharton and Gale from very modern MSS. Bede, though he speaks of the works of Aldhelm in terms of admiration, gives a very brief account of him. Malmesbury had before him a kind of common-place book written by King Alfred, which he quotes more than once for circumstances relating to Aldhelm, who seems to have been a favourite writer with that great monarch. Faricius says that there were, among the materials he used, some English documents, which he, as an Italian, calls "barbarice scripta."]

ALDHELM was born in Wessex, about the year 656. His father's name was Kenter, a near kinsman of King Ina; but a comparison of the dates is enough to show that Aldhelm was not, as Faricius states, King Ina's nephew. When but a boy (*pusio*), Aldhelm was sent to Adrian, abbot of Canterbury (Jan. 9), and soon excited the wonder even of his teachers by his progress in the study of Latin and Greek. When somewhat more advanced in years (*majusculus*), he returned to his native land of Wessex.

Near the beginning of the same century, an Irish monk named Maeldhu, which the Anglo-Saxons transformed into Meildulf, a voluntary exile from the land of his nativity, had taken up his abode among the solitudes of the vast forests which then covered the north-eastern districts of Wiltshire. He seems to have formed himself a cell amongst the ruins of an ancient British town. Maeldhu, after living for a short time as a hermit, found it necessary to secure for himself a less precarious subsistence by instructing the youths of the neighbouring districts; and thus the hermitage became gradually a seat of learning, and continued to be inhabited by Maeldhu's scholars after his death. People gave to the place the name of Meildulfes-byrig, which, softened down into Malmesbury, it still retains.

After his return to Wessex, Aldhelm joined this community of scholars, in imitation of whom he embraced the monastic life. His stay was not, however, of long duration; he made a second visit to Kent, and continued to attend the school of S. Adrian, until sickness compelled him to revisit the country of the West Saxons. He again sought the greenwood shades of Malmesbury; and after a lapse of three years he wrote a letter to his old master Adrian, describing the studies in which he was occupied, and pointing out the difficulties which he still encountered. This was in 680. From being the companion of the monks in their studies, Aldhelm soon became their teacher; and his reputation for learning spread so rapidly that the small society he had formed at Malmesbury was increased by scholars from France and Scotland. He is said to have been able to write and speak Greek, to have been fluent in Latin, and able to read the Old Testament in Hebrew. At this period the monks and scholars appear to have formed only a voluntary association, held together by similarity of pursuits and the fame of their teacher; and they do not appear to have been subjected to rules. How long they continued to live in this manner is uncertain; at a subsequent period, either at their own solicitation, or by the will of the West Saxon monarch and the bishop, they were formed into a regular monastery, and Aldhelm was appointed their abbot (circ. A.D. 683).[1]

Under Aldhelm the abbey of Malmesbury continued long to be the seat of piety as well as learning, and was

[1] A charter by Leutherius exists authorizing the foundation and appointing Aldhelm as its abbot, dated according to William of Malmesbury 675, according to the Malmesbury Chronicle 680; but it is almost certainly a forgery. See Wright: Biographia Brit. Literaria, I. p. 212.

enriched with many gifts by the West-Saxon kings and
nobles.   Its abbot founded smaller houses at Frome and
Bradford, in the neighbourhood.   At Malmesbury he found
a small but ancient church, then in ruins; this he rebuilt
or repaired, and dedicated it to SS. Peter and Paul, in that
age the favourite saints of the Anglo-Saxons.   His biographers have preserved the verses which Aldhelm composed
to celebrate its consecration.

Aldhelm may be considered the father of Anglo-Latin
poetry.   But he also composed in Anglo-Saxon.   King
Alfred placed him in the first rank of the vernacular poets
of his country; and we learn from William of Malmesbury,
that, even so late as the 12th century, some ballads he had
composed continued to be popular.   To be a poet, it was
then necessary to be a musician also; and Aldhelm's
biographers assure us that he excelled on all the different
instruments then in use, the fiddle and the pipes, &c.
Long after he became abbot of Malmesbury, he appears to
have devoted much of his leisure to music and poetry.
King Alfred entered into his note-book an anecdote which
is peculiarly characteristic of the age, and which probably
belongs to the period that preceded the foundation of the
abbey.   Aldhelm observed with pain that the peasantry,
instead of assisting as the monks sung mass, ran about from
house to house gossiping, and could hardly be persuaded to
attend to the exhortations of the preacher.   He watched
the occasion, and stationed himself in the character of a
minstrel on the bridge over which the people had to pass,
and soon collected a crowd of hearers, by the beauty of
his verse.   When he found that he had gained possession of
their attention, he gradually introduced, among the popular
ballads he was reciting to them, words of a more serious
nature, till at length he succeeded in impressing upon their
minds a truer feeling of religious devotion; " Whereas if,"

as William of Malmesbury observes, "he had proceeded with severity and excommunication, he would have made no impression whatever upon them." [1]

Few details of the latter part of Aldhelm's life have been preserved. We know that his reputation continued to be extensive. After he had been made abbot of Malmesbury, he received an invitation from Pope Sergius I. to visit Rome, and he is supposed to have accompanied Coedwalla, king of the West Saxons, who was baptized by that pope, and died at Rome in 689. Whether this be true, or not, Aldhelm's visit to Rome cannot be placed earlier than 688, because Sergius had been raised to the papal chair only in the December of the preceding year.

Aldhelm did not long remain at Rome. In 692, he appears, from his letter on the subject quoted by his biographers, to have taken part to a certain degree, though not very decidedly, with S. Wilfrid, in his great controversy against the Keltic usages of the Northumbrian Church. Soon after this, we find him employed in the dispute about the celebration of Easter with the Britons of Cornwall. A synod was called by King Ina, about 693, to attempt a reconciliation between the remains of the ancient British Church in the extreme west with the Anglo-Saxon Church, and Aldhelm was appointed to write a letter on the subject

---

[1] In after times Stephen Langton did something of the same sort. He sang a dancing-song and then moralized on it as his text. The sermon is preserved in the British Museum. This was the song, somewhat modernized in spelling :—

> "Belle Alez matin leva
> Son corps vesti et para
> Enz un verger s'en entra
> Cinq fleurettes y trouva,
> Un chapelet fit en a
>   de rose fleurie
> Par Dieu trahex vous en la
>   vous hinc aimez mie."

The mediæval preacher Maillard did much the same thing when preaching at Toulouse, singing at the top of his voice as a text the ballad "Bergeronette Savoisienne."

to Geraint, king of Cornwall, which is still preserved. We hear nothing further of the abbot of Malmesbury till the year 705, when, on the death of Hedda, the bishopric of Wessex was divided into two dioceses, of which one, that of Sherborne, was given to S. Aldhelm, who appears to have been allowed to retain at the same time the abbacy, and the other, Winchester, to one named Daniel.

Four years afterwards he died at Dilton, near Westbury, in Wiltshire, on the 25th May, 709. His body was carried to Malmesbury, where it was buried in the presence of Egwin, bishop of Worcester.

S. Aldhelm was not a voluminous writer. The works which alone have given celebrity to his name, are his two treatises on Virginity and his Ænigmata. It is impossible to admire their style. Even so far back as the 12th century, William of Malmesbury felt himself obliged to offer an apology for him, grounded on the taste of that age in which he lived. "The Greek language is involved, the Roman splendid, and the English pompous," is Malmesbury's account of the characteristics of these three languages. Certainly Aldhelm made English pomposity transpire through the splendour of Latin, which he involved like Greek.

ALDHELM, HILDELITH, AND THE NUNS OF BARKING

AN EARLY RELIQUARY.

S. CEDD, B. OF LONDON.

(A.D. 664.)

[English Martyrologies. His life is given by Bede, in his Ecclesiastical History, lib. 3, caps. 21, 22, 23.]

PEADA, son of Penda, King of Mercia, being appointed by his father King of the Midland English, by which name Bede distinguished the inhabitants of Leicestershire, and part of Lincolnshire and Derbyshire, from the rest of the Mercians; the young king visited Oswy, King of Northumbria, at Atwell, or Walton, was baptized along with several of his nobles, by Bishop Finan, and was provided by Oswy with two priests to instruct his people in Christianity. One of these was S. Cedd, who had been trained in the monastery of Lindisfarne. "When these two," says Bede, " travelling to all parts of that country, had gathered a numerous church to the Lord, it happened that Cedd returned home, and came to the church of Lindisfarne to confer with Bishop Finan; who, finding how successful he had been in the work of the Gospel, made him Bishop of the Church of the East Saxons, calling to him two other bishops, to assist at the ordination. Cedd, having received the episcopal dignity, returned to his province, and pursuing the work he had begun, with more ample authority, built churches in several places, ordaining priests and deacons to assist him in the work of faith, and the ministry of baptizing, especially in the city which, in the language of the Saxons, is called Ithancester,[1] as also in that named Tilabury (Tilbury); the first of which places is on the bank of the Pante, the other on the bank of the Thames; where, gathering a flock of servants of Christ, he taught them to observe the discipline of regular life, as far as those rude people were then capable.

[1] On the Blackwater; there is no city there now, but numerous traces of an ancient settlement, and an old chapel marks the site, in the parish of Bradwell.

"Whilst the doctrine of everlasting life was thus, for a considerable time, making progress, to the joy of the King and of all the people, it happened that the King, at the instigation of the enemy of all good men, was murdered by his own kindred. The same man of God, whilst he was bishop among the East Saxons, was wont also to visit, at intervals, his own country, Northumberland, to make exhortations. Ethelwald, the son of King Oswald, who reigned over the Deiri, finding him a holy, wise, and good man, desired him to accept some land to build a monastery, to which the King himself might frequently resort, to offer his prayers and hear the word, and be buried in it when he died ; for he believed that he should receive much benefit by the prayers of those who were to serve God in that place. The King had before with him a brother of the same bishop, called Celin, a man no less devoted to God ; who, being a priest, was wont to administer to him the word and the Sacraments, by whose means he chiefly came to know and love the bishop.

"That prelate, therefore, complying with the King's desires, chose himself a place to build a monastery among craggy and distant mountains, which looked more like lurking places for robbers, and retreats for wild beasts, than habitations for men. The man of God, desiring first to cleanse the place for the monastery from former crimes, by prayer and fasting, that it might become acceptable to our Lord, and so to lay the foundations, requested the King to give him leave to reside there all the approaching Lent, to pray. All which time, except Sundays, he fasted till the evening, according to custom, and then took no other sustenance than a little bread, one egg, and a little milk mixed with water. This, he said, was the custom of those of whom he had learnt the rule of regular discipline ; first, to consecrate to our Lord, by prayer and fasting, the places which they had newly received for building a monastery or a church. When there were ten days of Lent still remaining, there came a messenger to call him to the King; and he, that the religious work might not be intermitted, on account of the King's affairs, entreated his priest, Cynebil, who was also his own brother, to complete that which had been so piously begun. Cynebil readily complied, and when the time of fasting and prayer was over, he there built the monastery, which is now called Lestingan,[1] and established therein the religious customs of Lindisfarne."

At this time, owing to the influence of S. Wilfrid, who had been established at Ripon by Alchfrid, son of King Oswy, a great split was forming in the Church, which made itself felt even in the Royal family. All the missionaries of the north had been brought up in Iona, or Lindisfarne, and followed the Keltic ritual; Wilfrid, ordained by a French bishop, introduced Roman ways. Oswy had been baptized and educated by Keltic monks, and followed the usages of the Mother Church of Iona; but his wife, Eanfleda, had learned in exile Roman ways, and she brought with her to the court of Oswy a Canterbury priest—Romanus by name, and Roman in heart—who guided her religious exercises. Two Easter feasts were thus celebrated every year in the same house; and as the Saxon kings had transferred to the chief festivals of the Christian year, and especially to the Queen of Feasts, the meeting of assemblies, and the occasion which those assemblies gave them of displaying all their pomp, it is easy to understand how painful it must have been for Oswy to sit, with his earls and thanes, at the great feast of Easter, at the end of a wearisome Lent, and to see the Queen, with her maids of honour and her servants, persisting in fasting and penance, it being with her still only Palm Sunday.[2] To settle this difference, and prevent a rupture, the King

---

[1] Lastingham, near Pickering, in Yorkshire.　　[2] Bede iii. 25.

convoked a parliament at Whitby, in 664. In this parliament Colman, Bishop of Lindisfarne, Cedd, Bishop of the East Saxons, who had at this time re-established the episcopal see of London, and S. Hilda, the great abbess of Whitby, upheld the Keltic rite. On the other side were S. Wilfrid, the young Prince Alchfrid, and James, the deacon of York. In this parliament, it was decided that the Roman usages should be adopted, and Cedd renounced the customs of Lindisfarne, in which he had been educated, and returned to his diocese of London to spread the Roman usages there.

"Cedd," says Bede, "for many years had charge of his bishopric and of the monastery of Lastingham, over which he had placed superiors. It happened that he came there at the time that a plague was raging, and he fell sick and died. He was first buried in the open air, but in process of time, a church of stone was built in the monastery, in honour of the Mother of God, and his body was interred in the same, on the right hand of the altar."

The Bishop left the monastery to be governed after him by his brother Chad, who was afterwards made bishop. For the four brothers, Cedd, and Cynebil, Celin, and Ceadda (Chad)—which is a rare thing to be met with—were all celebrated priests of our Lord, and two of them also came to be bishops.

Lichfield Cathedral.

S. CHAD, B. OF LICHFIELD.

(A.D. 672.)

[Roman, Anglican, Scottish, and Irish Martyrologies. Authorities :—A life is given by Bede, lib. 3, cap. 23, 24, 28 ; Lib. 4, cap. 2, 3, also in a MS. printed in the Monasticon, and a Metrical Life attributed to Robert of Gloucester.]

S. CHAD or CEADDA was, perhaps, the youngest of the four brothers, Cedd, Cynebil, and Celin, all of whom were eminent priests. Our saint has sometimes been confounded with his brother Cedd, bishop among the East Saxons, whose life was related on January 7th. We know neither the date nor the place of his birth. It is certain he was an Angle, and a native of Northumbria, and that he flourished in the 7th century, though Dempster wishes to claim him as a Scottish, and Colgan as an Irish, saint. The date 620 A.D. has been suggested as the probable time of Chad's birth.

Bede tells us that S. Chad was a pupil of Aidan. That bishop required the young men who studied with him to spend much time in reading Holy Writ, and to learn by heart large portions of the Psalter, which they would require in their devotions.

At the death of Aidan, in 651, he went to Ireland, which was then full of men of learning and piety. The ravages of the Teutonic hordes on the continent had driven thither many illustrious foreigners. Then Ireland was fulfilling the mission ascribed to the Celtic race, that of supplying the link between Latin and Teutonic civilization. S. Chad, while in Ireland, made the acquaintance of Egbert, who was afterwards abbot of Iona.

Cedd had, at the request of Ethelwald, King of Deira, established a monastery at Lastingham, in Yorkshire. It stood just on the edge of that wide expanse of moorland which extends thirty miles inland from the coast.

Bishop Cedd returned thither from his diocese of London many years after, at a time when a plague was raging. He caught it, and whilst lying on his death-bed, bequeathed the care of the monastery to his brother, Chad, who was still in Ireland.

S. Chad, on his return, ruled the monastery with great care and prudence, and received all who sought his hospitality with kindness and humility. One day a stranger arrived at the gate, praying to be received into the brotherhood. This was Owini, lately steward of Queen Ethelreda. Tradition relates that as he pursued his toilsome journey from the fens which surrounded the abbey of Ethelreda into Yorkshire, the pilgrim erected crosses by the roadside to guide any burdened souls who might hereafter seek the same haven of rest. While quietly keeping the strict rule of S. Columba at Lastingham, our saint was summoned to the episcopate by King Oswy, of Northumbria.

But we must go back a little in our history. When the decision of the council or parliament, held at Whitby, in 664, was adverse to the Keltic rite, Cedd renounced the customs of Lindisfarne, but Colman, bishop of Lindisfarne, obstinately holding to them, withdrew from Northumbria into Scotland with all those who were willing to follow him. Tuda succeeded him in the pontificate of Northumbria, but died soon after.

"In the meanwhile," says Bede, "King Alchfrid (of Deira) sent Wilfrid the priest to the king of the Gauls, to have him consecrated bishop for himself and his subjects. Now he sent him to be ordained to Agilbert, of whom we said above that he left Britain, and was made bishop of the city of Paris. Wilfrid was consecrated, A.D. 665, by him with great pomp; many bishops coming together for that purpose in a village belonging to the king (Clothair III. of Neustria) called Compiegne. While he was still making some stay abroad, after his ordination, king Oswy, following the example of his son, sent to Kent a holy man of modest character, sufficiently well read in the Scriptures, and diligently carrying out into practice what he had learnt from the Scriptures, to be ordained bishop of the Church at York. Now this was a priest named Ceadda (Chad), brother of the most reverend prelate Cedd, of whom we have made frequent mention, and abbot of the monastery called Lastingham. The king also sent with him his own priest, Eadhed by name, who was afterwards, in the reign of Egfrid, made bishop of the Church of Ripon. But when they arrived in Kent, they found that Archbishop Deusdedit had departed this life, and that no other prelate was as yet appointed in his place. Whereupon they turned aside to the province of the West Saxons, where Wini was bishop, and by him the above-mentioned person was consecrated bishop; two bishops of the British nation, who kept Easter Sunday according to canonical custom from the 14th to the 20th day of the moon, being associated with him; for at that time there was no other bishop in all Britain canonically ordained, except Wini.

"Chad then, being consecrated a bishop, began at once

to devote himself to ecclesiastical truth and to chastity; to apply himself to the practice of humility, continence, and study; to travel about, not on horseback, but after the manner of the apostles, on foot, to preach the gospel in the towns, the open country, cottages, villages, and castles; for he was one of the disciples of Aidan, and endeavoured to instruct his hearers by the same actions and behaviour, according to his master's example and that of his own brother Cedd. Wilfrid also, who had already been made a bishop, coming into Britain, A.D. 666, in like manner by his doctrine brought into the English Church many rules of Catholic observance. Whence it came to pass that the Catholic institutions daily gained strength, and all the Scots that dwelt in England either conformed to these or returned into their own country."

This is Bede's account of the consecration of Wilfrid and Chad. At that time the diocese of York comprised the whole of Northumbria, including the south of Scotland. Under Oswald the see of Lindisfarne—the Iona of the Anglo-Saxons—was founded, containing within its jurisdicdiction the kingdom of Bernicia, until the establishment by Theodore of another see at Hexham. The writer of Wilfrid's life tells us that he objected to being consecrated by the English bishops, inasmuch as they were converts to the Scottish calculation regarding the celebration of Easter, or had received consecration from those who were of that opinion. Though Wini, who had been consecrated in Gaul, cannot be placed in either of these classes, yet Wilfrid knew he would summon to assist him two bishops who belonged to one of them; hence his preference for Gaul. Wilfrid's delay in Gaul, perhaps, excited the King's suspicions that he, like his friend Agilbert, was seeking a mitre there; or it may be that the king, influenced by the Scottish party (who could not forgive Wilfrid for the victory he gained over them at Whitby), consented to the election of Chad to the see.

Chad has been severely censured for accepting the bishopric under these circumstances. It may be, however, that he, stirred by sorrow at seeing the diocese left without a head, and doubting too, perhaps, whether Wilfrid would return, adopted this course, which may be condemned as uncanonical.

S. Chad is commemorated in some Breviaries as an archbishop. But he was only a bishop, for that dignity had fallen into abeyance from the time that Paulinus fled into Kent. But though no suffragans acknowledged Chad as their superior, he had ample scope for the most abundant energy. We have given above Bede's account of his untiring labours; let us now hear that of the metrical Life attributed to Robert of Gloucester.

He endeavoured earnestly, night and day, when he had thither come,
To guard well holy Church, and to uphold Christendom.
He went into all his bishopric, and preacht full fast,
Much of that folk, through his word, to God their hearts cast,
All afoot he travelled about, nor kept he any state,
Rich man though he was made he reckoned there of little great.
The Archbishop of York had not him used to go
To preach about on his feet, nor another none the mo,
They ride upon their palfreys, lest they should spurn their toe,
But riches and wordly state doth to holy Church woe.

Theodore, the new archbishop of Canterbury, arrived in England in A.D. 669. "Soon after," says Bede, "he visited the whole island, wherever the tribes of the Angles dwelt, for he was willingly entertained and heard by all persons; and everywhere he taught the right rule of life, and the canonical custom of celebrating Easter. He was the first archbishop whom all the English Church obeyed.

Visiting Northumbria, he charged Chad with not being duly consecrated. The saint replied with great humility,

" If thou knowest that I have not duly received the episcopate, I willingly resign the office, for I never thought myself
worthy of it ; but, though unworthy, I consented to under-
take it for obedience sake." Theodore hearing his humble
answer, said that he should not resign the episcopate, but
he himself completed his ordination again after the Roman
manner. He probably advised Chad to resign his see to
Wilfrid, for we next hear of our saint in retirement at
Lastingham.

In 669, Jaruman, bishop of the Mercians, died. King
Wulfhere asked Theodore to send them a bishop. The
archbishop did not wish to consecrate a fresh one, so he
begged King Oswy to let Chad, who was then at Lastingham, be their bishop. Theodore knowing that it was Chad's
custom to go about the work of the gospel on foot, rather
than on horseback, bade our saint ride whenever he had a
long journey to perform, but, finding Chad unwilling to
comply, the archbishop with his own hands lifted him on
horseback, for he thought him a holy man, and obliged him
to ride wherever he had need to go.

Though Chad was bishop of Lindisfarne for so short a
time, he left his mark on the affections of the people, for
we find that at least one chantry was dedicated in his name
at York Minster. Soon after his election to the bishopric
of the Mercians, he set out for Repton in Derbyshire,
where Diuma, the first bishop of the Mercians, had established his see.

Whether our saint desired a more central position for the
episcopal see, or was influenced by the wish to do honour
to a spot enriched with the blood of martyrs, Bede does
not tell us, but Chad established the Mercian see at Lichfield, then called Licetfield, or the Field of the Dead,
where one thousand British Christians are said to have been
put to death.

His new diocese was not much less in extent than that of Northumbria. It comprised seventeen counties, and stretched from the banks of the Severn to the shores of the German Ocean. Theodore, years afterwards, detached from it the sees of Worcester, Leicester, Lindesey (in Lincolnshire), and Hereford. Though it was far beyond the power of one man to administer it effectually, yet Bede witnesses that "Chad took care to administer the same with great rectitude of life, according to the example of the ancients. King Wulfhere also gave him land of fifty families to build a monastery at the place called Ad Barve, *i.e.*, 'At the wood,' in the province of Lindesey, wherein monks of the regular life instituted by him continue to this day." "Ad Barve" is conjectured by Smith, of Durham, to be Barton-on-Humber, where there is still standing a very ancient church, admitted by Rickman to be partly Saxon, dedicated to S. Peter.

After fixing his see at Lichfield, Bede tells us "he built himself a habitation not far from the Church, wherein he was wont to pray and read with seven or eight of the brethren, as often as he had any spare time from the labour and ministry of the Word. When he had most gloriously governed the Church in that province two years and a half, in the dispensation of the Most High Judge, there came round the time of which Ecclesiastes speaks. "There is a time to cast stones, and a time to gather them together," for a deadly sickness sent from heaven came upon that place, to transfer, by the death of the flesh, the living stones of the Church from their earthly abodes to the heavenly building. And after many of the Church of that most reverend prelate had been taken out of the flesh, his hour also drew near wherein he was to pass out of this world to our Lord. It happened that one day, Owini, a monk of great merit, the same that left his worldly mistress to become a subject of the heavenly king, at Last-ingham, was busy labouring alone near the oratory, where the bishop was praying, the other monks having gone to the Church, this monk, I say, heard the voice of persons singing most sweetly, and rejoicing, and appearing to de-scend from heaven. He heard the voice approaching from the south-east, till it came to the roof of the oratory, where the bishop was, and entering therein, filled the same and all about it. After a time he perceived the same song of joy ascend from the oratory, and return heavenwards the same way it came, with inexpressible sweetness. Presently the bishop opened the window of the oratory, and, making a noise with his hand, ordered him to ask the seven brethren who were in the church, to come to him at once. When they were come, he first admonished them to preserve the virtue of peace among themselves, and towards all the faithful, also to practise indefatigably the rules of regular discipline, which they had either been taught by him or seen him observe, or had noticed in the words or actions of the former fathers. Then he added that the day of his death was at hand : ' For,' said he, 'that amiable guest who was wont to visit our brethren, has vouchsafed to come to me also to-day, and to call me out of this world. Return, therefore, to the church, and speak to the brethren, that they in their prayers recommend my passage to the Lord, and that they be careful to provide for their own, the hour whereof is uncertain, by watching, prayer, and good works.' When they, receiving his blessing, had gone away in sorrow, Owini returned alone, and casting himself on the ground prayed the bishop to tell him what that song of joy was which he heard coming to the oratory. The bishop, bid-ding him conceal what he had heard till after his death, said, ' They were angelic spirits, who came to call me to my heavenly reward, which I have always longed after, and

they promised they would return seven days' hence, and
take me away with them.' His languishing sickness in-
creasing daily, on the seventh day, when he had prepared
for death by receiving the Body and Blood of our Lord,
his soul being delivered from the prison of the body, the
angels, as may justly be believed, attending him, he departed to the joys of heaven.

"It is no wonder that he joyfully beheld the day of his
death, or rather the day of our Lord, which he had always
anxiously looked for till it came; for notwitstanding his
many merits of continence, humility, teaching, prayer,
voluntary poverty, and other virtues, he was so full of the
fear of God, so mindful of his last end in all his actions,
that, as I was informed by one of the brothers, who instructed me in divinity, and who had been bred in his
monastery, whose name was Trumhere, if it happened that
there blew a strong gust of wind, when he was reading or
doing anything else, he at once called upon God for mercy,
and begged it might be extended to all mankind. If it
blew stronger, he, prostrating himself, prayed more earnestly.
But if it proved a violent storm of wind or rain, or of
thunder and lightning, he would pray and repeat Psalms in
the church till the weather became calm. Being asked by
his followers why he did so, he answered, 'Have ye not
read,—'The Lord also thundered in the heavens, and the
Highest gave forth His voice; yea, He sent out his arrows
and scattered them, and he shot out lightnings and discom-
fited them.' For the Lord moves the air, raises the winds,
darts lightning, and thunders from heaven to excite the
inhabitants of the earth to fear Him; to put them in mind
of the future judgment; to dispel their pride and vanquish
their boldness, by bringing into their thoughts that dreadful
time when, the heavens and the earth being in a flame, He
will come in the clouds with great power and majesty, to

judge the quick and the dead. Wherefore it behoves us to
answer His heavenly admonition with due fear and love.'

" Chad died on the second of March, and was first buried
by S. Mary's Church, but afterwards, when the Church of
the most Holy Prince of the Apostles, Peter, was built, his
bones were translated into it. In both which places as a
testimony of his virtue, frequent miraculous cures are wont
to be wrought. The place of the sepulchre is a wooden
monument, made like a little house covered, having a hole
in the wall, through which those that go thither for devotion
usually put in their hand and take out some of the dust,
which they put into water and give to sick cattle or men to
drink, upon which they are presently eased of their infir-
mity and restored to health."

We have told the life of S. Chad in the reverent language
of Bede, who, as he says, had some of the details direct
from those who had studied under the saint. Though
his episcopate was short, it was abundantly esteemed by the
warm-hearted Mercians, for thirty-one churches are dedicated in his honour, all in the midland counties, and either
in or near the ancient diocese of Lichfield. The first
church ever built in Shrewsbury was named after him, and
when the old building fell, in the year 1788, an ancient
wooden figure of the patron escaped destruction, which is
still preserved in the new church. The carver has represented him in his pontifical robes and a mitre, with a book
in his right hand, and a pastoral staff in his left.

His well is shown at Lichfield. There was one in London
called Chad's Well, the water of which was sold to vale-
tudinarians at sixpence a glass. Doubtless, from the miracles
alleged to have been wrought by mixing a little dust from
his shrine with water, he got the character of patron saint
of medicinal springs. At Chadshunt there was an oratory
and well bearing his name. The priest received as much

as £16 a-year from the offerings of pilgrims. Chadwell—one source of the New River—is, perhaps, a corruption for S. Chad's Well.

No writings of our saint have survived, but in Lichfield Cathedral library there is a MS. of the 7th century in Anglo-Saxon character, containing the Gospels of S. Matthew, S. Mark, and part of S. Luke, which is known by the name of *Chad's Gospel*.

Among the Bodleian MSS. there is an Anglo-Saxon homily for S. Chad's day, written in the *Middle Anglian* dialect, which stretched from Lichfield to Peterborough.

His relics were translated from the wooden shrine to the cathedral, when it was rebuilt by Bishop Roger, in honour of SS. Mary and Chad. In 1296, Walter Langton was raised to the see of Lichfield. He built the Lady Chapel, and there erected a beautiful shrine, at the enormous cost of £2,000, to receive the relics of S. Chad. This was spared by Henry VIII.

His emblem in the Clog Almanacks is a branch. Perhaps this was suggested by the Gospel, viz., S. John v., formerly read on the Feast of his Translation, which speaks of the fruitful branches of the vine. This translation was formerly celebrated with great pomp at Lichfield, on August 2nd.

As long as the virtues of chastity, humility, and a forsaking all for Christ's sake are esteemed among men, the name of the apostle of the Mercians ought not to be forgotten.

A beautiful legend formerly inscribed beneath the cloister windows of Peterborough, recorded the conversion of King Wulfhere's sons, Wulfade and Rufine, by S. Chad, and their murder by their father, for he had turned heathen again in spite of the entreaties of Queen Ermenild :—

By Queen Ermenild had King Wulfere
These twey sons that ye see here.
Wulfade rideth as he was wont,
Into the forest the hart to hunt ;
Fore all his men Wulfade is gone,
And sought, himself, the hart alone.
The hart brought Wulfade to a well,
That was beside Seynt Chaddy's cell.
Wulfade asked of Seynt Chad,
Where is the hart that me hath led ?
The hart that hither thee hath brought,
Is sent by Christ, that thee hath bought.
Wulfade prayed Chad, that ghostly Leech,
The faith of Christ him for to teach.
Seynt Chad teacheth Wulfade the feyth,
And words of baptism over him seyth.
Seynt Chad devoutly to mass him dight,
And hoseled Wulfade Christy's knight.
Wulfade wished Seynt Chad that day,
For his brother Rufine to pray.

The legend goes on to say that Rufine was baptized also by the saint. The king's steward, Werbode (who had been rebuked by the two princes for seeking the hand of their sister, Werburga), told Wulfere of their becoming Christians, and that they were then praying in S. Chad's oratory. The king took horse thither at once, and slew them both with his own hand. Stung with remorse, he fell ill, and was counselled by his queen to ask Chad to shrive him. As a penance the saint told him to build several abbeys, and amongst the number he completed Peterborough Minster, which his father had begun. This legend is told with very full and touching details in a Latin version printed in the Monasticon.[1]

The Latin version is this. King Wulfere, son of Penda the Strenuous, had been baptized many years before by B. Finan, and promised at the font, and again when he wedded

[1] Many of these details of S. Chad's life are taken from Mr. Warner's excellent life of S. Chad.

Ermenilda, of the royal house of Kent, to destroy all the idols in his realm. He neglected to do so, and let his three sons, Wulfade, Rufine, and Kenred remain unbaptized. His beauteous daughter, Werburga, had been dedicated to Christ as a virgin by the Queen; yet, when Werbode, his chief councillor, and the chief supporter of idolatry in the realm, sought her hand in marriage, the king consented. The queen, Ermenilda, however, sharply rebuked him for his presumption. The brothers threatened him with their sore vengeance if he again preferred his lowborn suit to their sister. Their disdainful words cost them dear.

While Chad was praying by a fountain near his cell, a hart, with quivering limbs and panting breath, leaped into the cooling stream. Pitying its distress, the saint covered him with boughs, then placing a rope round its neck, he let it graze in the forest. Wulfade came up, heated in the chase, and asked where the beast had gone. The saint replied, " Am I keeper of the hart? Yet, through the ministry of the hart I have become the guide of thy salvation. The hart bathing in the fountain foreshoweth to thee the laver of baptism, as the text says: As the hart panteth after the water-brooks, so panteth my soul after thee, O God."

Many other things did the saint set forth about the ministry of dumb animals to the faithful. The dove from the ark told that the waters were dried up.

The young prince replied, " The things you tell me would be more likely to work faith in me if the hart you have taught to wander in the forest with the rope round its neck were to appear in answer to your prayers." The saint prostrated himself in prayer, and lo! the hart burst from the thicket. The saint exclaimed, " All things are possible to him that believeth. Hear then, and believe the faith of Christ." The saint instructed him, and baptized him. The next day he received the Eucharist, and went home, and told his brother Rufine that he had become a Christian. The other said, "I have long wished for baptism; I will seek holy Chad." The brothers set out together. Rufine espying the hart with the cord round its neck, gave hot chase; the animal made for the saint's cell, and leaped into the fountain as before. Rufine saw a venerable man praying near. He said, "Art thou, my lord, father Chad, guide of my brother Wulfade to salvation?" He answered, "I am." The prince earnestly desiring baptism, Chad baptized him, Wulfade holding him at the font, after the manner taught by holy Church.

Then they departed, but returned daily to him. Werbode stealthily spied their ways and doings, and told their father that they had become Christians, and were then worshipping in Chad's oratory, adding that their conversion would alienate his subjects. The king set out in anger for the cell, the queen sending Werbode before to tell the princes of his approach, that they might hide. But Werbode only looked in at the window of the oratory, and saw them praying earnestly. He returned to the king, and told him that his sons were obstinate in their purpose of worshipping Christ. The king, pale with anger, rushed towards the oratory. He threatened them with his vengeance for breaking the laws of the land by becoming Christians, and bade them renounce Christ. Wulfade replied, "They did not want to break the laws, and that the king himself once professed the faith which now he renounced. They wished to retain his fatherly affection, but no tortures could turn them from Christ." The king rushed furiously upon him, and cut off his head. His brother, Rufine, fled, but his father pursued him, and gave him a mortal wound. Thus these two departed to celestial glory. Werbode was smitten with madness when they returned to the castle and told the murder in the ears of all. The queen buried her sons honourably in one stone tomb, and withdrew with her daughter, Werburga, to the monastery at Sheppey, and then to that of Ely.

The king, overcome with remorse, fell dangerously ill. The queen counselled him to seek out Chad, and confess to him. Wulfere took her advice, and starting one morning with his thanes, as if to follow the chase, his attendants got scattered from him, and he was left alone. Soon he espied the meek hart with the rope round its neck; he followed its track gladly, till he came to Chad's cell. The king, approaching the oratory, espied the saint saying mass; he dared not enter till he had been shriven. When the canon began, so great a light shone through the apertures in the wall, that priest and sacrifice were covered with such splendour that the king was nearly blinded by it, for it was brighter than that of the natural sun.

The saint knew what the king wanted, so when the office was ended he hastily put off his vestments, and, thinking to lay them upon the appointed place, unwittingly hung them upon a sunbeam, for the natural sun was now streaming through the window. He found the king prostrate before the door; raising him up he heard the penitent's confession, and enjoined him as a penance, to root out idolatry, and to found monasteries.[1] He then motioned to the king that he should enter the oratory and pray. Wulfere, chancing to lift up his eyes, with wonder saw the vestments hanging on the sunbeam. He rose from his knees, and, drawing near, placed his own gloves and baldric upon the beam, but they immediately fell to the ground. The king understood by this that Chad was beloved by the Sun of Righteousness, since the natural sun paid him such homage.

[1] The reader will here recall the account of Lancelot and the Sacring in the Tower by Joseph of Arimathæa, in the Morte d' Arthur.

S. CHAD.

CANTERBURY CATHEDRAL.

S. DUNSTAN, ARCHB. OF CANTERBURY.

(A.D. 968.)

[Sarum and York Kalendars. Roman Martyrology and modern Anglican Kalendar. Also in some Martyrologies on Sept. 7. Authorities :—A life by Bridferth the priest, a contemporary and eye-witness of much that he describes. He died about 980. Secondly, a life by Eadmer (d. 1124) ; thirdly, one by Osbern, monk of Canterbury, written shortly after 1070 ; and fourthly, a life by Osbert, a monk, in the 12th cent., of which only fragments exist. In addition to these are notices in the early Chroniclers of England, as the Saxon Chronicle, the Chronicle of Henry of Huntingdon, William of Malmesbury, &c.]

S. Dunstan was born in the first year of King Athelstan, in 925, if we may trust the Saxon chronicle, near Glastonbury, where his father, Heorstan, was a great Thane. His mother's name was Cynethrith. He was sent as a boy to the famous abbey of Glastonbury to be instructed. There he was attacked with brain fever, which made him so noisy in the dormitory that he was given into the charge of a

woman to nurse him. One night he started out of his bed
and ran out, beating the air as if he were driving off savage
dogs, rushed up a spiral staircase that led to the roof of the
church, ran out on the lead, and was seen balancing himself
on the sharp ridge. After a while he came down and
entered the church, where he dropped into a refreshing
sleep, and next morning when he awoke had no remem-
brance of his nocturnal exploit.

After a while he was introduced to the court of King
Athelstan, where he did not stay long, as he made some
enemies there. Indeed, his fellow pages, probably jealous
of the favour with which he was regarded by the king,
ducked him in a horse-pond, and set the dogs on him,
when he crawled out covered with mud. At court he fell
desperately in love with a beautiful and amiable girl, and
wished to marry her, but his kinsman, Alphege the Bald,
Bishop of Winchester, urged him to elect the life of self-
renunciation, and to become a monk. Dunstan sharply
answered that he preferred a pretty young wife, and her
loving society to the woollen (*bidentenus*) smock of a monk.
Not long after Dunstan was afflicted with a violent eruption
over his body, which was intolerably irritating, and made
him fear for his life. Then he resolved to renounce the idea
of marriage, and to become a monk. And he went to his
kinsman Alphege. Now one day Bishop Alphege was
dedicating the church of S. Gregory that had been newly
built in the city of Winchester, and towards evening, ere he
went away, the bishop said to Dunstan, "The hour of compline is come, say the office with me in the church." So
they went in both together, and after the first versicles they
put their heads together for their mutual confession,[1] and
then separated them for the absolution. And just at that

---

[1] "Jungentes. capita sua in unum : quo confessiones suas solita consuetudine
vicessim proderent."

moment down came a great stone between their heads, brushing the hair of each, but doing no harm to either. We should say that the masons had not done their work in the new church as thoroughly as might be. Birdferth the biographer says that evidently the devil had thrown it at Dunstan, but missed his aim.

At Glastonbury he made the acquaintance of S. Ethelfleda (April 13) who lived near the church and was old and infirm. Another lady of his acquaintance was a noble matron named Ethelbyra, who used to do needlework for the church and its ministers. Dunstan, who was skilful with his brush, painted a stole, and then took it to her to fill in with silk and precious stones; and as she was fond of music, and he was a skilful musician, he took with him his harp to sing and play to her whilst she embroidered his stole. But after dinner he hung up his harp against the wall, near the open window, as the lady was obliged to attend to her servants; and, to every one's astonishment, the harp played faint chiming chords of æolian music.[1] This astonished all, who looked upon the circumstance as a prestige of the future greatness and sanctity of the harper. The sound was, in fact, drawn out by the current of air setting the strings in vibration, as in the beautiful toy, the æolian harp.

Dunstan occupied his monastic life at Glastonbury in acquiring all the learning of the time, and he devoted himself as well to various arts useful for the service of the Church as music and painting, and he became especially skilful as a metal-worker. A MS. illuminated by his hand still exists in the British Museum. On the death of King Athelstan, Edmund the Magnificent, his brother, was elected king; and he recalled Dunstan to court. The saint went,

[1] The imagination of the hearers led them to detect in the harp music the melody of a well-known antiphon.

but again got into trouble with the courtiers and the king through the severity of his virtue, and was obliged to leave. One day, almost immediately after, the king was hunting a stag on the Cheddar (Ceoddir) hills, when the hart rushed to the edge of the rock and plunged over the precipice. The king was galloping with relaxed rein, and saw instantly his peril. "God help me, and I will bring Dunstan back !" and he drew in his rein. The horse rose in the air on its hind legs, and reeled back, and the king was saved. He instantly recalled Dunstan and said to him, "Quick, saddle your nag, and accompany me." Dunstan obeyed, wondering much at this change in the king's mood, and Edmund led the way in the direction of Glastonbury. After they had reached the abbey, Edmund entered the church and prayed ; then rising, he took Dunstan's hand, and leading him into the abbatial chair, seated him, and said, "Be thou the possessor and staunch defender of this throne, and whatever thou findest deficient for the conduct of Divine worship, I will supply out of my treasury."

This was in 943, and if we are to believe the date of his birth given by the Saxon Chronicle, and confirmed by Birdferth, he can only have been eighteen at the time Edmund died by the hand of Liofa at Pucklechurch in 946. The body of the murdered king was brought to Glastonbury, and was there buried by Abbot Dunstan.

King Edmund left two sons, Edwy and Edgar, but as they were very young, his brother Edred was chosen to succeed him. Edred was crowned at Kingston by Archbishop Oda, and was acknowledged by the Northumbrians, who, however, revolted in 948 or thereabouts, and chose Eric, son of Harold Blue-tooth, king of Denmark, to be their king. Edred marched against them and defeated them. During the war Dunstan persuaded him to send his treasures to Glastonbury to be under the care of the monks.

On the death of Ethelgar, bishop of Crediton in Devon, the king urged Dunstan to accept the vacant see, but he steadily refused. Edred died at Frome in 955, and was buried at Winchester. He was succeeded by Eadwig, or Edwy, the eldest son of King Edmund. He was still very young, only sixteen. His reign, like those of his father and uncle, was very short, and, unlike theirs, it was also very unlucky.

It is difficult to arrive at the truth of the events that occurred in the reign of King Edwy, both because the Saxon Chronicle is very short, and because all other accounts contradict one another so that one hardly knows what to believe. For S. Dunstan had by this time taken a very decided line, and this made two great parties in the Church and in the country generally ; one favoured his scheme of reform, and the other as vehemently opposed it. And as historians favoured one or other side, so is their history coloured. Edwy was the enemy of Dunstan ; therefore the admirers of Dunstan have tried to make out Edwy as bad as possible. On the other hand, most modern writers have a prejudice against S. Dunstan, and try to make the best of Edwy, and the worst of S. Dunstan. If the Saxon Chronicle gave us a full account we should know better what to believe. But as it is we must put the story together as well as we can by comparing the different accounts. The Chronicle does not tell us any harm of Edwy, and Ethelwerd and Henry of Huntingdon give him a good character, and lament his early death. On the other hand it is certain that he drove S. Dunstan out of the kingdom. Now when we see how well things went on both under Edred, and afterwards under Edgar, when S. Dunstan was again in power, and how badly they went on under Edwy, we shall think that Edwy did a very injudicious as well as blameworthy act in driving S. Dunstan away. Dunstan was unquestionably a great and wise minister, but it was very natural for several reasons that Edwy should dislike him.

S. Dunstan's great object was the reformation of the Church. Among the Anglo-Saxon clergy, before S. Dunstan, marriage was rather the rule, celibacy the exception. The clergy attached to the cathedrals lived under a kind of canonical rule, but were almost universally married. In the richer conventual foundations, ruled mostly by noble and warlike abbots, and noble abbesses, they took no vow of chastity; they married or remained unmarried at their will.[1] The only true monks were the Benedictines, who had been introduced by S. Wilfred. They were chiefly in the northern kingdoms, but throughout England their monasteries had been mercilessly wasted by the Danes; a white cowl was as rare as a ghost. When Dunstan began his career there were true monks only at Abingdon and Glastonbury. These things S. Dunstan and Bishop Ethelwald, of Winchester, and others who acted with them, set themselves heartily to reform. And besides, Dunstan was very anxious to get all the cathedrals and other great churches into the hands of monks instead of secular priests of any kind, whether married or not. This he succeeded in doing afterwards, under King Edgar, to a very great extent.

Now it could not but happen that different men should think very differently about changes like these. King Edred had been S. Dunstan's friend throughout, and had supported him in effecting his reform; but King Edwy took the other side. He does not appear to have been at all an enemy of the Church or a robber of monasteries, as some have made him out, for he was a benefactor of the churches both of

---

[1] "Monasteria nempe Angliæ ante Reformationem a Dunstano et Edgaro rege instituta, totidem erant conventus clericorum sæcularium; qui amplissimis possessionibus dotati et certis sibi invicem regulis astricti, officia sua in ecclesiis quotidie frequentarunt; omnibus interim aliorum clericorum privilegiis, atque ipsa uxores ducendi licentia gaudebant."—Wharton, *Anglia Sacra,* I. p. 218.

Abingdon and Glastonbury. But he did not like S. Dunstan, and did not approve of his schemes. So far from turning out secular priests to put in monks, he seems to have sometimes intruded secular priests into churches where there had always been monks. William of Malmesbury bitterly complains that secular priests were put into his own church at Malmesbury, making it what he calls "a stable of clerks," as if secular priests were no better than beasts· It is no wonder then that we find the whole history both of Edwy and Edgar perverted by party spirit. S. Dunstan's friends make out all the ill they can against Edwy, and S. Dunstan's enemies all the ill they can against Edgar. Hence both Edwy and Edgar are charged with crimes which most likely neither of them ever committed. As far as can be made out, it is most likely that Edwy, before he was chosen king, or directly after, married, or took to live with him—it is impossible to decide which—a beautiful young girl named Elgiva. She was so near of kin to him that according to the laws of the Church he could not lawfully marry her. Anyhow, this union caused great scandal and offence. Now on the very day of the coronation of Edwy, during the banquet, the king left the hall where were his nobles, bishops, and aldermen, and went into another room to visit his wife and her mother. This was resented by the guests as an insult, and they were very angry. S. Dunstan rose from his seat, and with the Bishop of London, pursued the king into the apartment of his wife, and insisted on his return. We may well believe that much strong language was used on both sides, and that neither Edwy nor Elgiva ever forgave S. Dunstan. It so happened that a party of the monks at Glastonbury were displeased at the changes effected by their abbot, and complained to the king. Edwy caught at the opportunity, and either in 956 or 957, S. Dunstan was driven out of the kingdom and took refuge in Flanders.

Now, either by the banishment of Dunstan, or his way of governing in general, Edwy gave great offence to his subjects. In 957 Mercia and all England north of the Thames revolted, and chose Edgar, the brother of Edwy, to be king. Edgar, king of the Mercians, as he is now called, at once sent for S. Dunstan to come to him, and presently gave him the bishopric of Worcester, and afterwards that of London. S. Dunstan held both these bishoprics at once, a thing clearly against the laws of the Church, and only perhaps justified by the necessities of the time. The next year, 958, Archbishop Oda, acting in concert with S. Dunstan, forced Edwy to separate from Elgiva. This we know from the Saxon Chronicle, and it looks very much as if the intercourse between the king and Elgiva was such as very generally to outrage the public sense of decency, so that Wessex was getting discontented as well as Mercia, and the only resource for Edwy, if he hoped to retain his crown, was to surrender Elgiva. It is difficult to decide what happened next. All we know for certain is that Archbishop Oda died the same year that he divorced Elgiva, and that Edwy died the year after, 959. But there are all sorts of stories, told by later writers, too readily accepted as true by prejudiced modern historians, which are so utterly contradictory and so confused as to their dates, that we may hope they are false. Some woman or other, by whom they mean Elgiva, was killed by the Mercians in their revolt; according to another account, Archbishop Oda had her branded in the face with a red-hot iron to destroy her seductive beauty, and then banished her to Ireland; and when she ventured to come back, Oda's men caught her at Gloucester, and cut the sinews of her legs, so that she died in this horrible way. Now it is clear that Elgiva could not have been killed in the revolt of Mercia, because she was divorced afterwards, and the other

dreadful tale rests on no contemporary authority.[1]   Some
say that Edwy was killed, but this is uncertain.   Anyhow
he died in 959, and was buried at Winchester.

On the death of Edwy, his brother Edgar, king of the
Mercians, was chosen king by the whole nation, and he
reigned over the West Saxons, Mercians, and Northumbrians.   He was only sixteen years old when he was
elected king.

It is almost as hard to write about Edgar as about his
brother, because the accounts which we have of him are
very contradictory.   The earliest and best writers glorify
him as the best and greatest of kings ; the Saxon Chronicle can hardly speak of him without bursting forth into
poetry.   On the other hand there is no king about whom
there are more stories to his discredit.   Here we can see
party spirit.   There is no doubt that under Edgar England
was wonderfully prosperous and wonderfully peaceful.
His chief adviser was S. Dunstan, and he was the great
friend of the monks.   This was enough to make one side
call him everything that was good, and the other side
call him everything that was bad.   Most likely he was
neither so good nor so bad as he is pictured.   But
the prosperity of his reign is certain, while the crimes
attributed to him are very doubtful.   They come mostly
from stories in William of Malmesbury, who allows that he
got them from popular ballads, the most untrustworthy of
all sources of history ; but some are on better authority.[2]
Archbishop Oda died a little time before King Edwy, and
in his place Elfsine, bishop of Winchester, was appointed.
But Elfsine set out to Rome to get his pall from the pope,
and died of cold in crossing the Alps.   In 959, the first

[1] It is first told by Osbern, who wrote about 1070.
[2] As Osbern, who relates the story of the outraged nun, for which S. Dunstan put
the king to penance.

year of King Edgar, Dunstan was chosen to the archbishopric of Canterbury,[1] and the next year he went to
Rome and got his pall from Pope John XII. For
the time Dunstan had all his own way, and he and
Ethelwald, bishop of Winchester, Oswald, bishop of Worcester, and others of their party, turned the secular priests
out of many of the chief churches of England, and put in
monks. Dunstan was the king's chief adviser, and the
laws of Edgar, his strict government, the peace and prosperity of England under him, and his authority over all the
other princes of Britain, speak for themselves, and we cannot
doubt the wisdom and prudence of the great counsellor.

That the cares of office in Church and State did not
prevent S. Dunstan from cultivating his darling art of
music appears from a pretty story told by his biographer.
One night the archbishop dreamt that he was at a royal
wedding feast, and was listening to the song of the
minstrels, when one of the harpers, a youth in white
raiment, came to him, and asked why he did not join in
the nuptial hymn. "Because I know not the words and
the strain," said the sleeper. Then the young harper
played and sang to him, "O Rex gentium dominator
omnium, propter sedem Majestatis tuæ da nobis indul-
gentiam, Rex Christe, peccatorum, Alleluia." On awaking
he repeated to himself the words and music, and calling
together the singers of Canterbury, taught them the antiphon, and committed it to writing, lest it should be forgotten. Nor did he forget his monks at Glastonbury, but
visited them and knew each personally, and not they only,
but all the little scholars in the monastery school.

One day Dunstan was at Bath, which he visited yearly

[1] On the day that he said mass for the first time in Canterbury Cathedral, a white
dove appeared fluttering over his head. The bird afterwards perched on Bishop
Odo's tomb.

for the sake of the hot springs. After dinner, falling into an abstracted mood, he saw one of the little boys of Glastonbury borne heavenward by angels. A day or two after a monk from Glastonbury came to Bath to see Dunstan. "How are all the brethren?" asked the abbot. "All are well," answered the monk. "What all?" again asked Dunstan." "All but one little fellow, a boy who is dead." "God rest his happy spirit," said S. Dunstan; "I have seen him borne by angels to everlasting peace."

Now Dunstan was the friend and counsellor of the king, whom he probably loved. But Edgar, if an excellent administrator of the laws, was not a man of peculiarly virtuous life. Some of the stories told of him are most probably false, but others must be true. Osbern, the biographer of S. Dunstan, says that the king had been guilty of a great crime. He had dishonoured a nun. Shortly after, Dunstan came into his presence. The king, as usual, extended his hand to him, but the archbishop, with flashing eye, folded his arms, and turned abruptly away, exclaiming, "I am no friend to the enemy of Christ."

The king, awed, threw himself at his feet. Then S. Dunstan bitterly reproached him, and he saw that Edgar was moved to true contrition; he laid on him a penance, that for seven years he was not to wear his crown, and was to fast twice in the week.

He was determined to enforce the celibacy of the clergy, and his efforts drew on him bitter hatred. "Let them live canonically or go out of the Church," said he. A gathering of both parties was held at Calne, in a large hall. The opposition was headed by a Scottish bishop called Heornel, or Bernal.[1] After a long altercation, Dunstan, now very aged, exclaimed, "We have wasted

---

[1] Hector Boece calls him Fothadh, and pretends that he obtained the victory over S. Dunstan.

much time in endless dispute ; I confess I cannot force you to obedience. But I appeal to Christ, to His judgment I commit the cause of His Church." Scarcely had he said the words than, with a crash, a portion of the roof fell on his opponents, and they escaped from the ruins bruised and with broken bones.

On the death of King Edgar, before another king could be chosen, there was a great movement against the monks. Elthere, alderman of the Mercians, and others, began to turn the monks out of several churches, and to bring back the secular canons with their wives. But Ethelwin, alderman of the East-Angles, whom men called "the Friend of God," gathered a meeting of the wise-men of his own earldom, and they determined to keep the monks, and they joined with Brithnorth, alderman of the East-Saxons, and assembled an army to defend the monasteries. Meanwhile there was a dispute who should be king. Both the sons of Edgar were very young ; Ethelred was about seven, Edward about thirteen. Of the two it was most natural to choose Edward, and King Edgar, before he died, had said that he wished it to be so. But some were in favour of Ethelred. An assembly was called for the election of a king. Then Dunstan took his cross, and leading Edward into the midst of the assembly, stood and demanded the throne for him. All bowed to the authority, and Edward was consecrated by the archbishop, in 975. The story of his death has been already told (March 18th). When Dunstan was called to crown Ethelred, in 979, as he placed the golden circle on the boy's brow, he said, if we may trust Osbern, "Since thou hast attained the kingdom through the death of thy brother, whom thy mother hath shamefully slain, the sword shall never depart from thy house, till it hath cut it off, and the crown shall pass to one of another race and language."

On the feast of the Ascension, in the year 968, S. Dunstan sang mass and preached to the people with singular unction. After he had returned to the altar to complete the sacrifice, he turned to give the benediction, and then again he addressed the people, and announced to them that he was about to die. After the conclusion of mass, he went to the refectory and dined, then returned to the church and pointed out the place where he desired to be laid. Three days after, he was no more.

In Art S. Dunstan is chiefly honoured by a foolish representation of the devil caught by the nose by a pair of blacksmith's pincers. The legend relates that Satan tempted him as he was at work at his forge, by assuming the form of a beautiful girl. Dunstan at once attacked him with his pincers and put him to flight.

S. EDMUND, K.M.

(A.D. 870.)

[Roman Martyrology. Notker, Wandelbert, Sarum, York, Hereford, and Anglican Reformed Kalendars. Authority :—A Life by Abbo of Fleury, written by command of S. Dunstan. Abbo died in 1004, he wrote in 980. The Life is in Surius.]

THE Anglo-Saxon Chronicle says, under date 870, " This year the army (of Danes) rode across Mercia, into East Anglia, and took up their winter quarters at Thetford. And the same winter King Edmund fought against them, and the Danes got the victory, and slew the king, and subdued all the land, and destroyed all the minsters which they came to. The names of their chiefs who slew the king were Hingwar and Hubba."

The Danes arrived in 866, when Edmund was king of East Anglia, Burhred of Mercia, and when Osbert had been deposed in Northumbria, and Ælla, who was not of the kingly house, had been set up instead. The first winter the Danes spent in East Anglia. In 867 they crossed the Humber and took York. In 868 they entered Mercia and extended their ravages as far as Nottingham. In 870 they invaded East Anglia, with which hitherto they had maintained peace, having probably been bought off by Edmund. A battle was fought, and in it Edmund fell. This is all that can be counted historical in what we are told of Edmund. But legend has greatly improved the story.

Roger of Wendover tells a story, founded probably on old ballads, to account for the invasion by the Northerners.

" There was, not long ago, in the kingdom of the Danes, a certain man named Lodbrog (Hairy-breeches), who was sprung from the royal race of that nation, and had by his

S. EDMUND. After Cahier.

wife two sons, Hingvar and Hubba. One day he took his hawk and went unattended in a little boat to catch small birds and wild-fowl on the sea coast and in the islands. While thus engaged he was surprised by a sudden storm, and carried out to sea, and after having been tossed about for several days and nights, was at last carried in sore distress to the English coast, and landed at Redham, in the province of Norfolk. The people of that country by chance found him with his hawk, and presented him as a sort of prodigy to Edmund, king of the East Angles, who, for the sake of his comely person, gave him an honourable reception. Lodbrog abode some time in the court of the monarch, and as the Danish tongue is very like English, he began to relate to the king by what chance he had been driven to the coast of England. The accomplished manners of King Edmund pleased Lodbrog, as well as his military discipline and the courtly manners of his attendants. Emulous of the like attainments, Lodbrog asked permission of the king to remain in his court, and having obtained his request, he attached himself to the king's huntsman, whose name was Bjorn, that he might with him exercise the hunter's art. But such was the skill of Lodbrog, that he was always successful in hunting or hawking, and being deservedly a favourite with the king, Bjorn became jealous of him, and giving way to deadly hatred, he one day, when they were hunting together, attacked him and slew him, and left his body in a thicket. This done, the wicked huntsman called off his dogs with his horn, and returned home. Now Lodbrog had reared a certain greyhound in King Edmund's court, which was very fond of him, and, as is natural, when the huntsman returned with his own dogs, remained watchful by his master's body.

" Next day, as King Edmund sat at table, he missed Lodbrog from the company, and anxiously asked his attendants what had befallen him; on which Bjorn, the huntsman, answered that he had tarried behind in a wood, and he had seen no more of him. But as he was speaking, Lodbrog's dog came into the hall and began to wag his tail and fawn on all, and especially on the king; who, on seeing him, said to his attendants, 'Here comes Lodbrog's dog; his master is not far behind.' He then began to feed the dog, hoping soon to see his master. But he was disappointed, for when the greyhound had satisfied his appetite, he returned to keep his accustomed watch over his master's body. After three days he was compelled by hunger to return to the king's table, and Edmund, greatly wondering, gave orders to follow the dog when he left the hall, and watch whither he went. The king's servants fulfilled his commands, and followed the dog till it led them to Lodbrog's lifeless body. On being informed of this the king was greatly disturbed, and directed that the body should be committed to a more honourable sepulchre. King Edmund then caused diligent inquisition to be made touching the death of Lodbrog; and Bjorn the huntsman was convicted of the crime, and by order of the king, the captains and wise men of his court passed sentence on him. The judges unanimously agreed that the huntsman should be put into the boat in which Lodbrog had come to England, and should be exposed on the sea without sail or oar, that it might be proved whether God would deliver him."

Roger of Wendover goes on to tell how Bjorn was wafted across to Denmark, and there was examined by torture by Hubba and Hingvar, sons of Lodbrog, who recognized their father's boat. Bjorn, under torture, declared that Lodbrog had been put to death by Edmund, king of the East Angles. The Danes accordingly assembled an army and invaded East Anglia, to avenge on Edmund the murder of their father.

The Norse story does not agree with this at all. According

to the Sagas, Ragnar Lodbrog was seized by Ælla, king of the Northumbrians, and was thrown into a dungeon full of serpents, in which he sang his dying song, the famous Krakumal. His sons, they say, were called Eirekr, Agnarr, Ivar, Bjorn Ironside, Hvitserkr and Sigurd Worm-in-the-eye.[1] Matthew of Westminster tells the tale, as does Roger of Wendover; both drew from the same source.

Edmund encamped at the royal vill of Haelesdune, when Hingvar and Hubba landed at Berwick-on-Tweed, and ravaged the country on their march through Northumbria. In 870 Hingvar entered East Anglia, and was attacked by Edmund whilst his force was divided from that of Hubba. Both sides suffered severely. Hubba joined Hingvar at Thetford, and the united army attacked Edmund again. His force was far outnumbered. He was routed, and he and Humbert, bishop of Elmham, were taken in a church; Humbert was despatched with the sword. Edmund was tied to a tree, and the Danes shot at him with their arrows, till they were tired of the sport, when he was decapitated, and his head flung into a thicket of the forest of Haelesdune (Hoxne). Next year, says the legend, when the Danes retired, the king's body was recovered and his head was sought in the wood. As those searching called in the wood to one another, asking where was the head, they heard a voice calling, " Here ! here ! here ! " and found it proceeded from the head, which lay among the brambles, guarded by a great grey wolf. It was buried at Beodricsworth, afterwards called Bury S. Edmunds.[2] Sweyn, in 1014, was about to burn and

---

[1] The Thattr af Ragnars Sonum says that Ingvar, who invaded Northumbria and fought Ælla, "had two brothers, sons of a concubine, one called Yngvar, the other Husti ; and these two put King Edmund to death by order of Ingvar."—Fornm. Sögur, i. 354.

[2] Roger of Wendover and Matthew of Westminster took their narrative of the martyrdom of S. Edmund from the Passion by Abbo of Fleury. He, however, does not tell the story of Lodbrog and Bjorn.

pillage the abbey of Bury, when he was suddenly struck ill and died, and this was attributed to the interposition of the saint.

[March 18

S. EDWARD, K. M.

(A.D. 978.)

[Anglican Martyrologies, also modern Anglican Kalendar. Roman Martyrology. The elevation of his body, June 20th ; his translation, Feb. 18th. Authorities :—The Chronicle of John of Brompton, Osbern of Canterbury, William of Malmesbury.]

IN the year 975, King Edgar died, and was buried at Glastonbury. He had been twice married. His first wife was the beautiful Ethelfleda, who died shortly after the birth of her son Edward. After her death Edgar married, in 964, Elfrida, daughter of Ordgar, earl of Devonshire, and she became the mother of two sons by him, Edmund, who died young, and Ethelred. As soon as king Edgar was dead, Edward, who was thirteen years old, a good youth, upright in all his dealings, and fearing God, was elected to the crown, much to the discontent of Elfrida, who desired to see her son Ethelred on the throne.

In the year 979, when Edward was aged seventeen, he was murdered. Now, certainly he was not a martyr for the Christian faith, nor for right and truth in any shape ; but he was a good youth, and was unjustly and cruelly killed, so people looked on him as a saint, and called him Edward the Martyr. The Anglo-Saxon Chronicle greatly laments his death, and says that a worse deed had never been done since the English came into Britain. It does not, however, say who killed him, but only that he was killed at eventide, at Corfe Castle. Henry of Huntingdon says that king

Edward was killed by his own people; Florence of Worcester, that he was killed by his own people by order of his step-mother, Elfrida. William of Malmesbury, in one part of his book, says he was killed by earl Elfhere, but this is improbable, as no reason for such an act appears. But in recording his death, Malmesbury attributes the crime to Elfrida, and tells the story thus :—

When Edward was elected, Elfrida hated him, because she wished her own son, Ethelred, to be king, and she ever sought how she might slay Edward. Now, one day the young king was hunting in Dorsetshire, hard by the castle of Corfe, where Elfrida and Ethelred her son dwelt. And the king was weary and thirsty, so he turned away alone from his hunting, and said, "Now will I go to rest myself at Corfe, with my step-mother Elfrida, and my brother Ethelred." So king Edward rode to the gate of the house, and Elfrida came out to meet him, and kissed him. And he said, "Give me to drink, for I am thirsty." And Elfrida commanded, and they brought him a cup, and he drank eagerly. But while he drank, Elfrida made a sign to her servant, and he stabbed the king with a dagger ; and when the king felt the wound, he set spurs to his horse, and tried to join his comrades, who were hunting. But he slipped from his horse, and his leg caught in the stirrup, so he was dragged along till he died, and the track of his blood showed whither he had gone. And Elfrida bade that he should be buried in Wareham, but not in holy ground, nor with any royal pomp. But a light from heaven shone over his grave, and wonders were wrought there. But when the child Ethelred heard of his brother's murder, he began to cry and bewail him, for Edward had always been very kind to the little boy. His mother, stung by her conscience, and angry with him for his lamentations, rushed on the child to beat him, and having no stick at hand, she pulled a wax candle out of its socket, and thrashed him with it. But afterwards, when she heard of the mighty works which were done at the grave of king Edward, how the sick were healed, and the lame walked, she resolved to go and see the miracles with her own eyes. But when she mounted her horse to ride, the horse would not stir. So Elfrida's hard heart was shaken, and she became alarmed about her sin that she had committed, and she retired into the convent of Wherwell, that she might repent in ashes the wickednes she had done. The body was afterwards translated to the minster at Shaftesbury (June 20th).

S. Edward is usually drawn with a youthful countenance, having the insignia of royalty, with a cup in one hand and a dagger in the other. Sometimes he has a sceptre instead of the cup; and at other times a falcon, in allusion to his last hunt.

MURDER OF S. EDWARD.

S. EGWIN, OF WORCESTER, B. C.

(ABOUT 720.)

[The life of S. Egwin was written by his contemporary, S. Britl:wald, Archbishop of Canterbury. This original has not descended to us, but a fragment of a somewhat later recension of this life exists; and a still later life, probably an amplification of that by Brithwald. Moreover, S. Egwin is mentioned by Matthew of Westminster, Florence of Worcester; William of Malmesbury also speaks of him in his Acts of the English Bishops.]

S. EGWIN was of the royal blood of the Mercian kings, and was born at Worcester, in the reign of Ethelred and Kenred. He was elected Bishop in 692. By his zeal in rebuking the illicit connexions formed by some of the great men in his diocese, and vehemence in reforming the corrupt morals of all, he stirred up a party against him, and with the connivance of the King, he was expelled his diocese. Egwin, meekly bending to his fate, determined to make a pilgrimage to Rome. According to a popular mediæval legend, he also resolved to expiate at the same time certain sins of his youth, by putting iron fetters on his feet, which were fastened with a lock, and he cast the key into the Avon. As he neared Italy, on a ship from Marseilles, a huge fish floundered upon deck, and was killed and cut open; when, to the surprise of the Saint, in its belly was found the key to his fetters. He accepted this as an expression of the will of heaven, and released his limbs. According to another version of the story, the fish was caught in the Tiber, after S. Egwin had appeared before the Pope in Rome; but William of Malmesbury doubts the whole story as an idle legend.

After his return, with the assistance of Kenred, King of Mercia, S. Egwin founded the famous abbey of Evesham, under the invocation of the Blessed Virgin. After this he undertook a second journey to Rome, in company with

Kenred, and Offa, King of the East Saxons.　S. Egwin died
on the 30th December, 717, and was buried in the monastery
of Evesham.　　The translation of his relics probably took
place on Jan. 11th, on which day many English Martyrologies mark his festival.

S. EGWIN, BISHOP OF WORCESTER, After Cahier.

ENAMELLED CHEST, which contained the remains of King Ethelbert.

S. ETHELBERT, K. C.

(A.D. 616.)

[Roman, Ancient Anglican and German Martyrologies, that of Usuardus, &c. Authority :—Bede, lib. i. c. 11-15, 25, 26 ; lib. ii. c. 5.]

S. ETHELBERT was son and successor of Irmenric, king of Kent, and great grandson of Hengist, the first of the Saxon conquerors of Britain. He reigned for thirty-six years over the oldest kingdom of the Heptarchy—that of Kent—and gained over all the other Saxon kings and princes, even to the confines of Northumbria, that kind of military supremacy which was attached to the title of Bretwalda, or temporary chief of the Saxon Confederation. His wife was Bertha, daughter of Charibert, son of Clovis, king of France; a Christian princess, who brought over with her as chaplain, one Lethard or Liudhard, of Senlis, a bishop, who exercised his ministry in a church formerly built, in Roman times, near the walls of Canterbury, and dedicated to S. Martin. Tradition records the gentle and lovable virtues of queen Bertha, but little is known of her life; she has left but a brief and uncertain illumination on those distant and dark horizons, over which she sits like a star, the herald of the sun. Her example and the virtues of Liudhard probably did much to break up the ground in the heart of Ethelbert; but his conversion was reserved for the coming and preaching of S. Augustine and his companions, the missioners sent from Rome by Gregory the Great. These landed first in the Isle of Thanet, which joins close to the east part of Kent, and thence they sent a message to king Ethelbert, saying why they had come into his land. The king sent word back to them to stay in the isle till he fully made up his mind how to treat them; and he gave orders that they should be well taken care of in the meanwhile. After some days he came himself into the isle, and bade them come and tell him what they had to say. He sat under an oak, and received them in the open air, for he would not meet them in a house, as he thought they might be wizards, and they might use some charm or spell, which, according to the superstition of the time, was held to be powerless out of doors. So they came, carrying a silver cross, and a picture of Our Lord painted on a wooden panel, chanting in procession the litanies in use at Rome, in the solemn and touching strains which they had learnt from Gregory, their spiritual father, and the father of religious music. At their head marched Augustine, whose lofty stature and patrician presence attracted every eye, for, like Saul, "he was taller than any of the people from his shoulders and upwards."[1] The king, surrounded by a great number of his followers, received them graciously, and made them sit down before him. After having listened to the address which they delivered to him and to the assembly, he gave them a loyal, sincere, and, as we should

---

[1] Gotselinus: Vita S. Aug. c. 45.

say in these days, truly liberal answer. "You make fair speeches and promises," he said, "but all this is to me new and uncertain. I cannot all at once put faith in what you tell me, and abandon all that I, with my whole nation, have for so long a time held sacred. But since you have come from so far away to impart to us what you yourselves, by what I see, believe to be the truth and the supreme good, we shall do you no hurt, but, on the contrary, shall show you all hospitality, and shall take care to furnish you with the means of living. We shall not hinder you from preaching your religion, and you may convert whom you can." So he gave them a house to dwell in, in the royal city of Canterbury, and he let them preach openly to the people, of whom they quickly brought some over to the faith, moved by the innocence of their lives, and the sweetness of their heavenly doctrine, which was confirmed by miracles. They were given, as Bede tells us, the Church of S. Martin in which "to sing, to pray, to say mass, to preach, and to baptize." But it was not long before the king also submitted to the truth, and was baptized; and before the year was out, there was added to the Church more than ten thousand souls. It was on Whitsun-Day, in the year of grace, 497, that the English king entered into the unity of the Holy Church of Christ. Since the conversion of Constantine, excepting that of Clovis, there had not been any event of greater moment in the annals of Christendom. Then the king told Augustine and his companions that they might build new churches, and repair the old ones which Christians had used before the Saxons invaded England, and drove the ancient Church into Cornwall and Wales. Ethelbert, faithful to the last to that noble respect for the individual conscience, of which he had given proof even before he was a Christian, was unwilling to constrain any one to change his religion. He allowed himself to show no preference, save a deeper love for those who, baptized like himself, became his fellow-citizens in the heavenly kingdom. The Saxon king had learnt from the Italian monks that no constraint is compatible with the service of Christ.[1] It was not to unite England to the Roman Church, but it was in order to tear her from it, a thousand years after this, that another king, and another queen, Henry VIII., and his cruel daughter Elizabeth, had to employ torture and the gallows.

From the time of his conversion, Ethelbert behaved for the twenty remaining years of his life, as became a good king and a good Christian. He gave his royal palace in Canterbury for the use of the archbishop, founded Christ Church in Canterbury, S. Andrew's in Rochester, S. Paul's in London, and built and endowed the abbey and church of SS. Peter and Paul without the walls of Canterbury, commonly called S. Augustine's; and was instrumental in bringing over to the faith of Christ, Sebert, king of the East Saxons, with his people, and Redwald, king of the East Angles. The former remained true to Christ till his death; but Redwald returned, at least in part, to the worship of Thor and Wodin. Ethelbert died in the year 616, and was buried in the Church of SS. Peter and Paul, near the body of his devout queen Bertha, and the holy prelate Liuthard. A light was always kept burning before his tomb by our pious ancestors.

Liuthard of Senlis, the chaplain of queen Bertha, is also commemorated on this day.

---

[1] "Didicerat enim a doctoribus auctoribusque suæ salutis, servitium Christi voluntarium, non coactum esse debere." Bede i. 26.

ENAMELLED CHEST, which contained the remains of King Ethelbert.

S. ETHELWOLD, B. OF WINCHESTER.

(A.D. 984.)

[Found in post-mediæval Martyrologies. In an Anglican Kalendar, published by Martene T. VI., Wilson, Menardus, Wyon, Greven, Molanus, the Bollandists, a Mass in honour of S. Ethelwold is published by Mabillon, and the Bollandists. Authority :—A life by Wulstan, Abbot of Winchester, a contemporary, d. 990, "in Latin prose, in a style below mediocrity," *Wright*, but interesting, and thoroughly trustworthy. Also, William of Malmesbury, "De Pontif. Anglic."]

ETHELWOLD, or Ethelwald, whom his contemporaries and followers designated as the "father of monks," was a native of Winchester, the son of a noble citizen of that place. He was born in the reign of Edward the Elder, and, therefore, not later than the year 925; and was trained to learning from his childhood.

While very young he was taken to court, and his talents

and many good qualities obtained for him the favour of King Athelstan, and of the learned men who enjoyed the favour of that monarch. He received the tonsure at the hand of Alphege the Bald, Bishop of Winchester.

Ethelwold appears to have been nearly of the same age as Dunstan; they were ordained to the priesthood at the same time; and when Dunstan became abbot of Glastonbury, towards 943, Ethelwold took the monastic habit, and became the companion of his studies and of his counsels. He then qualified himself as a grammarian and poet, entered eagerly into the deepest mysteries of theology; and probably followed all the various pursuits in the arts and sciences, to which Dunstan showed so much attachment. Ethelwold is said to have been an ingenious mechanic, and an early writer of the abbey of Abingdon mentions two bells which he made with his own hands.

Ethelwold remained but a few years at Glastonbury, for before the end of the reign of Edred, who died in 955, he was seized with the desire of visiting France, and of perfecting himself in learning and monastic discipline in the schools and monasteries which flourished in that country. But the queen-mother, Edgiva, a woman of great piety, represented to King Edred the loss his kingdom would sustain if he allowed such an eminent monk to leave it; and when Ethelwold applied for leave to travel, he met with a refusal.

As an excuse for retaining him in England, the king gave him the abbey of Abingdon, in Berkshire, a small monastic house, then deserted and in ruins, which the king and his mother at the same time enriched with lands, and other valuable gifts. Ethelwold induced five monks of Glastonbury, Osgar, Foldbirht, Friwegar, Ordbirht, and Eadric, to accompany him, and they began to erect a new building, more worthy of the purpose for which it was destined. This work was not completed till the beginning of the reign of Edgar, when Ethelwold sent Osgar to Fleury to be instructed in the monastic discipline of that place, and qualified to teach it to the monks of Abingdon.[1]

There was at Abingdon a simple monk named Ælfstan, who was employed by Ethelwold in the kitchen. Ælfstan had no easy time of it; he had to cook for the monks, and cook for the workmen engaged on the buildings of the new monastery. He was an active, neat, punctual man, who had always meals ready at the right time, the kitchen swept scrupulously clean, the pots and pans scrubbed, and set in their places. Ethelwold had no idea that Ælfstan was without assistance in the kitchen; by some oversight he had not supplied him with a scullery-monk, but the cheerful, dapper cook did not complain, but went about his work singing and making melody in his heart to God.

One day Ethelwold came into the kitchen and found the great cauldron full of bread and meat stewing for the work-men, the floor as clean as a platter, no dusters scattered here and there, and dirty bowls in the sink, on the table, or crumbs everywhere, but all in perfect, scrupulous order.

"Oh, my brother! thou art a gallant soldier of Christ!" exclaimed the abbot. "Thrust thy hand into the cauldron, and fish me up a crust from the bottom, and see if the Lord approveth thee, as I do."

The obedient Ælfstan took the lid off the simmering copper, put in his arm through the steam, down through the boiling water, and brought up a dripping crust. And his arm was uninjured. "Tell no man," said the abbot, rejoiced.

Ælfstan, the cook, became eventually Abbot of Abingdon, and afterwards Bishop of Winchester.[2]

---

[1] The most detailed account of Ethelwold's works at Abingdon will be found in the extracts from the register of that house, printed by Dugdale in his Monasticon, vol. i.

[2] Elsewhere called Alfsin or Elfsige; he occupied the episcopal throne of Winchester from A.D. 1015 to 1032.

Ethelwold was a mighty builder, never at rest unless superintending and setting his hand to the construction of new buildings ; and several times in jeopardy thereby. One day a great beam fell on him whilst he was helping the masons ("the devil seeking to extinguish him," says Wulstan), and knocked him head over heels into a ditch, where it lay across him. All his ribs were broken, and but for the ditch it would have crushed the life out of him.

In 963, about three years after the completion of the monastery at Abingdon, King Edgar promoted Ethelwold to the bishopric of Winchester, left vacant by the death of Brithelm. He was consecrated by S. Dunstan, then Archbishop of Canterbury, on the first Sunday in Advent, November 29th, the vigil of S. Andrew's Day.

Ethelwold had no sooner been advanced to the bishopric of Winchester, than he joined Dunstan in the great revolution in the Anglo-Saxon Church, which the archbishop had at heart. He found his cathedral served by secular married priests, canons under no strict rule, living with their wives and families near the great church, feeding well, and sometimes taking the convivial glass, chirpy, jovial, worthy souls, very unlike the grave, austere, enthusiastic monks in the abbeys. Not only the Old Minster at Winchester—the monastery attached to the episcopal see—was occupied by these convivial, married canons, but also the New Minster, formed by King Alfred. The former was immediately under the jurisdiction of the bishop ; and having obtained the authorization of Edgar, in the second year of his bishopric (A.D. 964), he ejected the priests, their wives and children from the close, and invited his monks from Abingdon to occupy their stalls, and enjoy their emoluments.

The last mass sung by the old canons was on the first Saturday in Lent. The mass ended, they were singing the communion, when the western door was opened by the arriving black-robed swarm from Abingdon. The words of the communion were : " Serve the Lord in fear and rejoice unto him with reverence, receive discipline, lest ye perish from the right way." The monks thought the words appropriate. Osgar, turning in the sunshine at the great gate, exclaimed, " My brethren ! the canons are calling us to come in and take their places. Why tarry ye without ?"

Then an officer of the king stood forth, and ordered the canons to assume the black, monastic robe, or to depart. The canons, bewildered, filled with dismay—the plans of Ethelwold were apparently kept secret till the blow fell—fled from the church, to collect such of their property as they would be suffered to carry off.[1] Three only consented to turn their wives and children out of their houses on the world, and embrace the religious life. " At this time," says Wulstan, " there were no monks in England save at Glastonbury and Abingdon."

The New Minster soon shared the fate of the Old, and within the same year the secular priests were expelled from Chertsey and Milton—old monasteries which had been gradually invaded by clergy not living under rule, who had brought in with them their wives and children to disturb the silent cloisters.

These vigorous proceedings caused great irritation in the diocese between the old clergy and the new monks, and the biographer of Ethelwold does not hesitate to charge the former with an attempt to poison their prelate at his own table, because after a draught of home-made wine he felt uncomfortable internally.[2]

[1] " He drave out the clergy of the bishopric, because they would not take the rule, and he set there monks in their room." Saxon Chron. sub. ann. 983.

[2] The only ground for this charge is that the bishop had a pain in his stomach after drinking some home-made wine. He was none the worse for it, however, next day. That, Wulstan thinks, was a miracle. But he tells us elsewhere that the saintly bishop was subject to pains in the bowels. " Vir Dei infirmabatur frequenter in visceribus."

Having thus reformed the four monasteries above mentioned, and compelled the Nuns' Minster at Winchester to adopt a stricter rule, Ethelwold turned his attention to the monasteries which had been deserted during the Danish wars, and the possessions of which had fallen into the hands of the king. This was the case with most of the larger monastic foundations, and it assisted in no slight degree his favourite project of introducing monks in place of the secular clergy throughout the land. Ethelwold first bought from the king the ancient nunnery of Ely, and having, by the purchase of numerous estates, and by other gifts, made it " very rich," he placed in it a company of monks under an abbot named Brithnoth.[1] He bought and rebuilt, in the same manner, the ruins of Medeshamsted (Peterborough), and Thorney ; and he did not desist from prosecuting his great design until he had established monks in every part of England.

These extensive operations afforded Ethelwold frequent occasions for indulging in his love of the arts. One of his chief architectural works was the rebuilding the cathedral of Winchester, which occupied him some years, and was not finished till the year 980, when, on the 20th of October, it was consecrated with much pomp by Archbishop Dunstan, in the presence of King Ethelred and nine bishops. In the course of this undertaking Ethelwold disinterred the bones of S. Swithun, which he deposited in a new tomb in the interior of the church in A.D. 971.

Ethelwold was likewise skilful in the mechanical arts, and in music, taking after his old friend and fellow pupil, Dunstan. We have already mentioned the bells which he made with his own hands for the abbey of Abingdon. From the early register of the same abbey we learn that he also

---

[1] Saxon Chron. sub. ann. 963. A detailed account of Ethelwold's benefactions to the minster of Ely is found in MS. Cotton, Vespas. A. xix.

made "a .certain wheel full of bells, which he called the Golden Wheel, on account of its being plated with gold, which he ordered to be brought out and turned round on feast days to excite greater devotion." He is said to have been eminent as a mathematician; and a treatise on the quadrature of the circle, addressed by him to the celebrated Gerbert, is still preserved.

Under Ethelwold's superintendence the monastery of Winchester became an eminent school, which produced many of the most remarkable bishops and abbots of the following age. His biographer describes to us the eagerness with which he employed himself in the instruction of youth, and the pleasure he appeared to feel when teaching children the grammar and metres of the Latin language, and reading to them Latin books in English.

He suffered from a tumour on his thigh, and from pains in the bowels, yet he would not eat meat, except for three months, and in his last sickness, at the exhortation of S. Dunstan.

One night a monk named Theodric went to him when the time came for rising to sing the praises of God, and found that instead of having gone to bed after Compline the bishop had sat up reading by a candle he held in his one hand, whilst he shaded his eyes with the other. This was a novel idea to Theodric. How a man could find such delight in a book as to forget his sleep for it was to him amazing. That a man should read by candlelight was a novelty. So he took the candle from the bishop's hand, drew the book towards himself, and tried to read. But his eyes ached next day, and never, till his dying day, did Theodric afterwards approve of study by candlelight.

Another night the old bishop fell asleep over his studies, and the candle he held dropped on the parchment page. He was found by a monk with his head bowed and the candle on the book, and though the grease had swaled over the page the parchment was unconsumed. This was regarded as miraculous.

The chief literary work of S. Ethelwold (or, at least, the one by which he was best known) was a translation into Anglo-Saxon of the Rule of S. Benedict. This work he is said to have undertaken at the desire of King Edgar, who gave him for it the manor of Southbourne, which he immediately conferred upon his foundation of Ely. Ethelwold's munificence appeared in the number and richness of his endowments, probably far exceeding those of any other individual in his age. His charity was exhibited in a no less remarkable manner ; when his own diocese was suffering under the visitation of famine, he ordered all the sacred vessels of the Church to be broken up and turned into money, observing that the precious metals were better employed in feeding the poor than in ministering to the pride of ecclesiastics. The Saxon Chronicle calls him "the well-willing bishop." Ethelwold died on the 1st of August, 984, and was buried in the cathedral of Winchester. S. Dunstan was present at his death.

The church of Alvingham in Lincolnshire is dedicated to him under the name of Adwell, which is a corruption of Ethelwold.

S. ETHELBURGA, V. ABSS.

(7TH CENT.)

[Anciently venerated in Essex, an office for her with nine lections in MS. in the Cotton Library. Authority :—Bede, in his Eccl. Hist., and a life in Capgrave.]

S. ETHELBURGA was born in Lindsey in the village of Stalington; she was the daughter of Offa, and sister of S. Earconwald, Bishop of London. Her father was not baptized, and he resented the infantine piety of his daughter, and combated angrily her resolution to devote herself to a life of virginity. Bathed in tears after a violent outbreak of her father's wrath, Ethelburga would steal away to the little church where she had been baptized; and Ethelburga's path in the hottest summer is ever green, and green also in winter to this day, says her biographer.

Finding that her father was determined to marry her to a man of wealth and position, she fled to Barking in Essex, accompanied by one maid. She arrived there in harvest and was given shelter by a farmer, on condition that she should assist in reaping. She knelt, and lo! angels with sickles swept down the golden corn whilst she prayed.

S. Earconwald, consecrated Bishop of London in 675 by S. Theodore of Canterbury, having come into his paternal inheritance, founded a religious house at Chertsey, in Surrey, for men, and one for women at Barking, over which he placed his sister Ethelburga as first abbess.

Whilst Barking Abbey was being built, a beam was

brought for the roof which, when fitted, was found too short. Then Earconwald took one end and Ethelburga the other, and pulled it out to the proper length.

As Barking was the first religious house for women founded in England, Earconwald sent for the holy woman, Hildelitha, who had been brought up in a French convent, to assume the direction.

A pestilence swept away the priests who ministered at the altars of the convent and carried off many of the nuns. This was in 664. Consternation fell on the survivors. But one night as the sisters went from their church, at the end of matins, to pray at the graves of the clergy who had preceded them into the other world, they saw all at once the whole sky lighted up and cover them all as with a radiant shroud. It was a flash of summer lightning which their imaginations transformed into a luminous gravecloth flung across the sky above their heads. They were so terrified that the hymn they were singing died on their lips. By this mysterious light they saw the graveyard illumined, and noticed that there was abundance of space for many graves. They understood that this flash of light showed them the place where their bodies must lie, and revealed at the same time to them the glory into which their souls would gaze.

There was a nun at Barking, named Theoritgytha, who, after having been long the humble and zealous assistant of Ethelburga, was warned of the death of the abbess, her friend, by a vision, in which she saw her dear Ethelburga wrapped in a shroud which shone like the sun, and raised to heaven by golden chains, which represented her good works. Ethelburga died shortly after. Deprived of her spiritual mother, Theoritgytha lived for nine years in the most cruel sufferings, in order, says Bede, that the furnace of this daily tribulation might consume all the imperfection that remained among her many virtues. At last paralysis assailed all her

members, and even her tongue. Three days before her
death she recovered sight and speech ; she was heard to ex-
change some words with an invisible visitor. It was Ethelburga, who had come to announce her deliverance to her.

" I can scarcely bear this joy ! " said the sick woman ; and
the following night, freed at once from sickness and from the
bondage of the flesh, she entered into everlasting blessedness.

S. Ethelburga of Barking is not to be confounded with
S. Ethelburga of Lyming, widow of King Edwin.

S. Guthlac overcoming evil spirits.
(Harl. Roll Y. 6)

S. GUTHLAC, P.H.

(A.D. 714.)

[Anglican and Roman Martyrologies, the Monastic Martyrologies of Wyon and Menardus, etc. Authorities:—A life by Felix,

IN the days of Ethelred, king of the Mercians, there was a nobleman of Mercia, called Penwald; he belonged to the oldest and noblest family, called the Iclings. He was in worldly things wealthy, and when he was wealthiest he desired to take to himself a wife. He chose from the multitude of maidens the one who was fairest, and of the noblest kin; she was called Tette. And they were together until the time that God ordained that the woman became with child. Now after the child was born, on the eighth day, it was brought to the holy laver of baptism, and a name was given him from the appellation of the family and the clan, Guthlac. When the age came that the child should speak in child-fashion, he was no whit dull, nor disobedient to his parents in their commands, nor to those who nurtured him, either elder or younger. Nor was he addicted to boyish levities, nor to the vain talk of vulgar men, nor to unseemly fawning, nor lying flattering. Nor did he study the various cries of fowls, as childish age is often wont. But he grew up in sharpness, and was blithe in countenance, and pure and clean in his disposition, and innocent in his ways. After a time, when his strength waxed and he grew up to manhood, then he thought on the strong deeds of the heroes, and of the men of yore. Thereupon as though he had woke from sleep, his disposition changed, and he collected a great troop of his companions and equals, and himself took weapons. Then wreaked he his grudges on his enemies, and burned their city, and ravaged their farms, and widely through the land made much slaughter, and slew and took from men their goods. It was about nine years that the blessed Guthlac was thus engaged in hostile raids. But it happened one night when he had come from an expedition, as he rested his weary limbs, and thought over what he had done, he was suddenly inspired with divine awe, and his heart glowed with spiritual love; and when he awoke he thought on the old kings who were of yore, who, thinking of the wretched end of sinful life, forsook this world, and he saw all his ambition vanish on a sudden. And filled with godly fear, he vowed that if God would spare him till the morrow he would be His servant. When the darkness of night was gone, he arose and signed himself with the mark of Christ's rood. Then he bade his companions find another captain, and he told them that he would thenceforth be the servant of Christ. When they heard these words, they were greatly astonished, and begged him not to perform the things he had said. But he cared not for their words. God's love so burnt within him, that not only did he despise the world, but also he forsook his parents' home and wealth, and even his companions, and set all his hope on Christ. And after that he went to the monastery of Repton, and there received the tonsure, under the abbess Elfrida. And after he had assumed the monastic habit, he would taste no fermented liquor. Therefore the brethren hated him; but soon after, when they perceived the sincerity of his mind, and the cleanness of his life, they all loved him. He was in figure tall, and trim in body, winsome in mood, and goodly of countenance; he was mild and modest in his talk, and he was patient and humble, and ever in his heart divine love was hot and burning. When he had been two years in the monastery, he had learned the psalms, canticles, and hymns, and prayers, after Church order. Then he began to long for the wilderness and a hermitage. So he begged leave of the elders that he might depart.

One district only in Mid-England was desolate enough

to attract those who wished to be free from the world, viz., the great fens north of Cambridge ;[1] and there, accordingly, as early as the seventh century, hermits settled in morasses now so utterly transformed that it is difficult to restore in one's imagination the original scenery.

The fens in the seventh century were probably very like the forests at the mouth of the Mississippi, or the swampy shores of the Carolinas. Their vast plain is now, in summer, one sea of golden corn ; in winter, a black dreary fallow, cut into squares by stagnant dykes, and broken only by unsightly pumping mills and doleful lines of poplar trees. Of old it was a labyrinth of black wandering streams ; broad lagoons ; morasses submerged every spring-tide ; vast beds of reed and sedge and fern ; vast copses of willow, alder, and grey poplar, rooted in the floating peat, which was swallowing up slowly, all-devouring, yet all-preserving, the forests of fir and oak, ash and poplar, hazel and yew, which had once grown on that low, rank soil, sinking slowly (so geologists assure us) beneath the sea from age to age. Trees, torn down by flood and storm, floated and lodged in rafts, damming the waters back upon the land. Streams, bewildered in the flats, changed their channels, mingling silt and sand with the peat moss. Nature, left to herself, ran into wild riot and chaos more and more, till the whole fen became one "Dismal Swamp," in which, at the time of the Norman Conquest, Hereward, the "Last of the English," took refuge from the invading tyrants.

[1] This is the description of it by Felix: "There is in Britain a fen of immense size, which begins from the river Grant (the Cam), not far from the city named Grantchester (near Cambridge). There are immense marshes, now a black pool of water, now foul running channels, and also many islands, and reeds, and hillocks, and thickets, and with manifold windings wide and long it continues up to the North Sea." The following picturesque sketch of the great Cambridgeshire fens is from the pen of Mr. C. Kingsley, "The Hermits." It is given, as the lives of such as S. Guthlac and S. Botolph cannot be understood without the scenes in which they acted being brought clearly before the eye.

For there are islands in the sea which have escaped the destroying deluge of peat moss,—outcrops of firm and fertile land, which in the early Middle Age were so many natural parks, covered with richest grass and stateliest trees, swarming with deer and roe, goat and boar, as the streams around swarmed with otter and beaver, and with fowl of every feather, and fish of every scale.

Beautiful after their kind were those fair isles in the eyes of the monks who were the first settlers in the wilderness. The author of the " History of Ramsey" grows enthusiastic, and somewhat bombastic also, as he describes the lovely isle, which got its name from the solitary ram who had wandered thither, either in extreme drought or over the winter ice, and, never able to return, was found feeding among the wild deer, fat beyond the wont of rams. He tells of the stately ashes, most of them cut in his time, to furnish mighty beams for the Church roof; of the rich pastures painted with all gay flowers in spring; of the " green crown" of reed and alder which encircled the isle ; of the fair wide mere, now drained, with its " sandy beach" along the forest side; " a delight," he says, " to all who look thereon."

In like humour William of Malmesbury, writing in the first half of the twelfth century, speaks of Thorney Abbey and its isle. " It represents," says he, " a very paradise ; for that in pleasure and delight it resembles heaven itself. These marshes abound in trees, whose length, without a knot, doth emulate the stars. The plain there is as level as the sea, alluring the eye with its green grass, and so smooth that there is nought to trip the foot of him who runs through it. Neither is there any waste place ; for in some parts are apples, in others vines, which are either spread on the ground, or raised on poles. A mutual strife there is between Nature and Art, so that what one produces not, the other supplies. What shall I say of those fair buildings, which 'tis so wonderful to see the ground among those fens upbear?"

So wrote William of Malmesbury, after the industry and wisdom of the monks, for more than four centuries, had been at work to civilize and cultivate the wilderness. Yet even then there was another side to the picture; and Thorney, Ramsey, or Crowland, would have seemed, for nine months every year, sad places enough to us comfortable folk of the nineteenth century. But men lived hard in those days, even the most high-born and luxurious nobles and ladies; under dark skies, in houses which we should think, from darkness, draught, and want of space, unfit for felons' cells. Hardly they lived, and easily were they pleased; and thanked God for the least gleam of sunshine, the least patch of green, after the terrible and long winters of the Middle Ages. And ugly enough those winters must have been, what with snow and darkness, flood and ice, ague and rheumatism; while through the dreary winter's night the whistle of the wind and the wild cries of the waterfowl were translated into the howls of witches and demons; and the delirious fancies of marsh-fever made those fiends take hideous shapes before the inner eye, and act fantastic horrors round the fenman's bed of sedge.

Now when S. Guthlac found out the wilderness, he inquired of those who lived on the edge of the fen where he might find land that would serve him as a home. There was a man named Tatwin, who said that he knew an island which oftimes men had attempted to inhabit, but none had succeeded, on account of manifold horrors and fears, and the loneliness of the wide wilderness. When Guthlac heard these words, he bid him straightway shew him the place, and he did so; he embarked in a boat, and they rowed through the wild fens till they came to the spot called Crow

or Croyland, which was so lost in the marsh that few knew
of it except Tatwin, who had shewn it him. It was on S.
Bartholomew's Day that Guthlac came crashing through the
reeds of the morass to the island which was to be thenceforth his home for life.

When he had been there a few days, he was able to see
what things he needed for settling there, and he resolved to
return to Repton, and salute his brethren, for he had gone
away from them without taking leave. So in the morning
he went back to the monastery, and there he remained
ninety nights, and then returned to the beloved wilderness
with two servants. He was six-and-twenty years of age
when, endowed with heavenly grace, he first settled in the
wilderness.

Soon after he had settled there, he was tormented at
nights by strange sights and noises. He saw hairy figures
leaping about his island, and talking in British. His
imagination caused him to regard them as devils, but there
can be no doubt as to who they were, some of the old
British who had been driven by the Saxon invaders into
these wilds, where they dwelt among the islets of the vast
morass, unmolested, as in after years Saxons took refuge in
them from the Normans ; and these resented the intrusion
of the hermit, and endeavoured to scare him away, and
even had recourse to violence for that purpose.[1] His
imagination invested these islanders with fantastic terrors ;
and we read in the life by Felix how they "filled the house
with their coming, and poured in on every side, from above,
and from beneath, and everywhere. They were in countenance horrible, and they had great heads, and a long

[1] There can, I think, be no question about this. Felix introduces the account by
saying that this was at a time when the British, "the enemies of the Angle race,"
were annoying the English in various contests. Guthlac, the biographer informs
us, "understood the language of these accursed spirits speaking British, because
he had been erewhile in exile among them."

neck, and a lean visage; they were filthy and squalid in
their beards, and they had rough ears, and crooked 'nebs,'
and fierce eyes, and foul mouths; and their teeth were like
horses' tusks; and their throats were filled with flame, and
they were grating in their voices; they had crooked shanks,
and knees big and great behind, and distorted toes, and
cried hoarsely with their voices; and they came with im-
moderate noise and immense horror, that he thought that
all between heaven and earth resounded with their voices.
. . . And they tugged and led him out of the cot, and led
him to the swart fen, and threw and sunk him in the muddy
waters. After that they brought him into the wild places
of the wilderness, among the thick beds of brambles, that
all his body was torn. . . . After that they took him and beat
him with iron whips, and after that they brought him on
their creaking wings between the cold regions of the air."

S. Guthlac found on the island a great "law" or burial
mound, of old British times, which some men had broken
into in hopes of finding treasure. On the side of the
mound was a hole in which water stood. Beside this
Guthlac erected his hermitage. Then he resolved that he
would use neither woollen nor linen garment, but that he
would wear only clothing of skins; and so he continued to
do. Every day he ate barley bread and drank water.
One day the British devils endeavoured to persuade him to
abandon the use of bread except on one day in seven; but
Guthlac saw through the ingenious scheme whereby they
sought to rid the islet of his presence, and persisted in his
daily consumption of barley bread.

The biographer of S. Guthlac goes on to relate how one
Beccel, who acted as his servant, was shaving the saint one
day, when there fell on him a great temptation. Why
should he not cut S. Guthlac's throat, and instal himself in
his cell, that he might have the honour and glory of saint-

hood? But S. Guthlac perceived the inward temptation, which is told with the naïve honesty of those half-savage times, and rebuked the offender into confession, so that all went well to the end.

But there are gentler and more human touches in that old legend. One may read in it how all the wild birds of the fen came to S. Guthlac, and he fed them after their kind; how the ravens tormented him, stealing letters, gloves, and what not, from his visitors; and then, seized with compunction at his reproofs, brought them back, or hanged them on the reeds; and how, as Wilfrid, a holy visitant, was sitting speaking with him in his island, "there came suddenly two swallows flying on, and behold they raised up their song rejoicingly; and after that they sat fearlessly on the shoulders of the holy man Guthlac, and then lifted up their song; and afterwards they sat on his bosom, and on his arms and his knees. When Wilfrid had long wondering beheld these birds, he asked him wherefore the wild birds of the wilderness so submissively sat upon him. The holy man Guthlac answered him, 'Hast thou never learnt, brother Wilfrid, in Holy Writ, that with him who has led his life after God's will, the wild beasts and wild birds are tame?'" At length, after fifteen years in the fen, God was pleased to call His servant to Himself. It happened that he was in his chapel at his prayers, when he was attacked with illness. Beccel came to him and asked what ailed him. Guthlac answered slowly, and drew his breath with difficulty, "The meaning of my illness is this, that the spirit must be taken away from this body." When Beccel heard this, his tears burst forth. Then Guthlac comforted him, saying, "My son, be not thou grieved, for to me it is no sorrow to go to my Lord and God." When after four nights, Easter arrived, Guthlac in his sickness performed service to God, and sang mass, for he had been ordained priest, and after he had offered the precious sacrifice, he began to preach to Beccel, "and he penetrated him so deeply with his counsel that he never before or after heard the like." When the seventh day of his illness came Beccel arrived at the sixth hour of the day to visit him. He found him leaning in the corner of his oratory, against the altar. He could not speak to him at first, for, as he saw, S. Guthlac was in pain. But presently the holy man raised his weary limbs from the wall, and said, "My son, now it is very near the time, and do thou attend to my last commands. After my soul departs from the body, go to my sister Pegge[1] and tell her that I would not see her in life, that we might meet in heaven, before the face of God; and bid her place my body in the leaden coffin, and wind it in the sheet which Ecgburh the abbess sent me, and lay it in the coffin that holy virgin gave me." When he had thus spoken, he leaned his head against the wall, and uttered a long drawn sigh.

And on the following night, when Beccel fell to his nightly prayers, it seemed to him that the whole house was encompassed about with a great brightness, and the light remained till day. When it dawned on the morrow, the man of God stirred again a little, and raised up his weary limbs. Then he said to Beccel, "My son, prepare thyself to go on a journey which I bid thee; for now is the time for my spirit to leave these aching limbs and depart to endless joy." When he had said this, he stretched out his hands to the altar, and strengthened himself with the Body and Blood of Christ. And after that he raised his eyes to heaven, and stretched out his arms, and was dead.

After his death there arose on the place sanctified by the life and death of Guthlac a church with a community of monks, till at last, founded on great piles driven into the

[1] See Jan. 8.

morass, arose the lofty wooden abbey of Crowland, "at the estuary of four rivers," with its dykes, parks, vineyards, orchards, rich plough lands, from which, in time of famine, the monks of Crowland fed all the people of the neighbouring fens, with its tower with seven bells, an abbey which became a place of sanctuary for all who fled from tyranny and slavery.

Those who took refuge in S. Guthlac's place from cruel lords must keep his peace towards each other, and earn their living like honest men, safe while they so did; for between those four rivers S. Guthlac and his abbot were the only lords; and neither summoner, nor sheriff of the king, nor armed force of knight or earl, could enter—"the inheritance of the Lord, the soil of S. Mary and S. Bartholomew, the most holy sanctuary of S. Guthlac and his monks, the minster free from worldly servitude, the special almshouse of most illustrious kings, the sole refuge of any one in worldly tribulation, the perpetual abode of the saints, the possession of religious men, specially set apart by the common council of the realm; by reason of the frequent miracles of the holy confessor S. Guthlac, an ever-fruitful garden of camphire in the vineyards of Engedi; and, by reason of the privileges granted by the kings, a city of grace and safety to all who repent."

The great and good work begun by the monks was carried on by others whom they had pioneered, as by Richard de Rulos, Lord of Deeping (the deep meadow), who resolved to do the same work from the hall of Bourne, which the monks did from their cloisters; and having got permission from the Croyland monks, for twenty marks of silver, to drain as much as he could of the common marshes, shut out the Welland by strong dykes, built cottages, marked out gardens, and tilled fields, till "out of slough and bogs accursed he made a garden of pleasure."

One other lasting work those monks of Crowland seem to have done, besides those firm dykes and rich corn lands of the Porsand, which endure unto this day. For within two generations of the Norman conquest, while the old wooden abbey, destroyed by fire, was being replaced by that noble pile of stone whose ruins are still standing, the French abbot of Crowland sent French monks to open a school under the new French donjon, in the little Roman town of Grante-brigge, whereby—so does all earnest work grow and spread in this world, infinitely and for ever—S. Guthlac, by his canoe voyage into Crowland Island, became the spiritual father of the University of Cambridge in the Old World; and therefore of her noble daughter, the University of Cambridge, in the New World, which fen-men sailing from Boston deeps colonized and Christianized 800 years after S. Guthlac's death.[1]

S. MILBURGH, V. ABSS.

(7TH CENT.)

[Milburgh or Milburga is inscribed in the Roman Martyrology, and in that bearing the name of Bede. Authority :—William of Malmesbury and Capgrave.]

PERHAPS no higher commendation can be passed upon Domneva, the saintly wife of Merewald, than this, that she was the mother of three eminent saints, Milburgh, Mildred, and Mildgytha. S. Milburgh was the eldest, if the names are mentioned according to the order of birth, and this being most probably the case, the date of her birth would be about the year of grace, 662. We are told that from her earliest years she dedicated herself to God with all the ardour of her soul. Whatever she did, she did it for the love of Christ alone, endeavouring always to please Him, and to grow up in His holy service. The world, which would have many attractions to a highborn maiden, she thoroughly despised, and even life itself she counted as nothing, unless it were spent in entire devotion to God. That she might live such a life with greater freedom, and in holy companionship with others, moved by the same heavenly desire, she founded a monastery for religious virgins at Wenlock, in Shropshire. Wenlock Magna it was afterwards called, and Much Wenlock at the present day. Her father, and her uncle Wulfhere, king of Mercia, assisted her in this pious undertaking, and the monastery was endowed with ample possessions, many precious relicts of saints, and great privileges. Milburgh was consecrated abbess by Archbishop Theodore, and under her gentle rule the monastery became like a paradise in which Our Lord had planted the fairest flowers, and the sweetest fruits; and among them all S. Milburgh was pre-eminent in every virtue, and more especialty did the grace of humility shine forth in her. But the more she humbled herself, so much the more did God manifest His power in her by many gifts, enabling her to restore sight to the blind, and life to the dead. Her exhortations, full of heavenly unction, and the teaching of her saintly life, had a marvellous effect in bringing many souls from the darkness of error to the light of truth; and from the death of sin to a life of righteousness. Among the many wonderful things related of her, we read, that one day she went on some good errand to a village called Stoke, (Stoke S. Milburgh), when she was seen by the son of some neighbouring king, who wished to carry her

S. MILBURGH. After Cahier.

off by force, that he might marry her.   He got together a
few soldiers, and formed a plan for intercepting her; but
she, divinely admonished of the wicked scheme, fled at once
with a companion she had with her.   On her way she
crossed a shallow stream called the Corve.   As soon as the
rash man heard of her flight, he followed in great haste, but
when he came to the stream, the water suddenly rose, and
rendered further pursuit impossible; so Christ's lamb
escaped, while he stood still, confounded and amazed.

One night she had continued longer than usual in prayer
and contemplation, and, overcome with fatigue, fell asleep ;
nor did she awake till the rays of the morning sun fell
upon her.   Then she started up so suddenly that the
sacred veil fell from her head, but a slanting sunbeam
caught it ere it touched the ground, and held it suspended
in mid-air until she had time to rouse herself.   Then she
perceived the divine manifestation, and gave thanks to God,
praising and magnifying Him.

Upon another occasion, when she was alone in her
oratory, a widow came in carrying her dead child, and fell
down at the feet of the holy virgin, and with many tears
implored her to intercede for her, that her child might be
restored to life.   Milburgh rebuked her for making such a
strange request, and recommended submission to the divine
will.   "Go," she said, "and bury thy dead, then prepare
to follow thy son, for man is born to die."   But the widow
refused to go.   "No, I will not leave thee, unless thou restore my child to life."   When the holy virgin saw the
woman's faith, she prostrated herself in prayer by the body
of the child.   Immediately she was surrounded by fire,
which came down from heaven, and so entirely enve-
loped her, that it seemed impossible that she could escape
being consumed by it.   One of the sisters coming in, cried
out to her to fly, but she had no sooner spoken, than

all trace of fire was gone, and S. Milburgh, rising from her knees, presented the now living child to his mother.

S. Milburgh is represented as having authority over the birds of the air, and protecting crops from their ravages. In the parable, the fowls that came and devoured the good seed, were, we know, evil spirits.

After many years spent in good works and holy exercises, she was further purified and fitted, by long and painful illnesses, for those eternal mansions for which her soul longed. When the time of her departure drew near, she called together the whole community, and exhorted them all to have ever before them those two heavenly sentences : " Blessed are the pure in heart, for they shall see God. Blessed are the peacemakers, for they shall be called the children of God." She then recommended them to choose the most pious of the sisters for their future abbess. Taking leave of them, she said, " Most dear sisters, I have loved you as my own bowels, and have been over you, as a mother over her children, with pious care. A higher call now in mercy invites me, I go the way of all flesh, and commend you to God and the Blessed Virgin." Having armed herself for her passage with the holy sacraments, she gave up her pure soul into the hands of her Maker, on Feb. 23rd, 722, and was buried with honour near the altar, in the church of the monastery.

The monastery was afterwards destroyed by the Danes, and, in course of time, all trace of the tomb of the saint was lost. But many ages after, when it was being re-built by some Cluniac monks, two boys who were playing there, fell through the pavement, and sunk down to their knees in the ground. This accident occasioned some surprise, and the monks had the ground opened, and found human bones in the very foundation of the altar. An odoriferous exhalation, as of a most precious balsam, perfumed the whole church when the tomb was opened, and numerous miracles are said to have taken place at the tomb of the saint; so many, that of all the crowds who went to it, none came away without receiving some benefit. On May 26th, 1501, the relics were enclosed in a costly chest, and deposited in a conspicuous and eminent place in the same monastery, where they remained till its destruction in the time of Henry VIII.

Some ruins of the abbey church, built in the year 1080, may still be seen at Wenlock. They consist of south aisle and transept, and part of the cloister, sufficient to shew the magnificence of the ancient building.

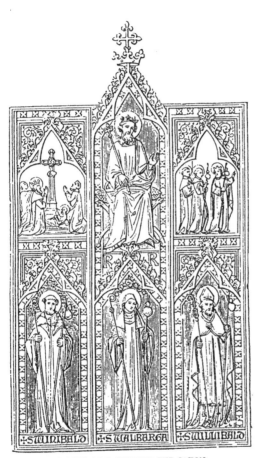

FAMILY OF S. RICHARD THE SAXON.
S. WALBURGA, Virg. Abbess.
S. WUNIBALD, Abbot.   S. WILLIBALD, Bishop.

From a Drawing by A. Welby Pugin.

S. SEXBURGA, Q. ABSS.

(A.D. 699.)

[Not in the ancient Latin Martyrologies. But by some modern Martyrologists, the Bollandists, Wyon, Bucellinus, Menardus, Greven, Molanus. Not in Sarum or York Kalendars, but probably on this day at Ely. Authorities :—Mention in the life of her sister, S. Etheldreda, and in the Historia Eleensis.]

ANNA, king of East Anglia, of the race of Uffa, and successor of the saintly Sigebert, fell on the battle-field before the ferocious heathen Penda, king of the Mercians (A.D. 654). Anna had married the sister of S. Hilda, the celebrated abbess of Whitby,[1] and by her had three daughters and a son. Those three daughters were saints, scarcely less illustrious than their aunts— Sexburga, Etheldreda, and Withburga.

Sexburga, the eldest, married Ercombert, king of Kent, the one who, after Ethelbert, showed himself most zealous for the extension of the Gospel. It was she who moved him to destroy the last idols which remained in his kingdom. After twenty-four years of conjugal life she became a widow (A.D. 664), and was regent for four years of the kingdom of her son Egbert. She had two daughters, Ermenilda and Earcongotha, both numbered with the saints. Ermenilda married Wulphere, king of the Mercians, in 658, and was left a

---

[1] This is not quite certain. According to other accounts Hereswitha, sister of S. Hilda, was married not to Anna, but to his brother Ethelhere.

widow in 675, when she retired as a nun to Sheppey, and died third abbess of Ely.

Earcongotha became abbess of Faremoutier, in Brie, and died in 700. Ermenilda was the mother of S. Werburga, fourth abbess of Ely.

As soon as Egbert was old enough to reign, in 668, Sexburga resigned the regency, and taking the veil from the hands of Archbishop Theodore of Canterbury, founded a monastery in the isle of Sheppey, at the mouth of the Thames, separated from the mainland by that arm of the sea in which S. Augustine, on Christmas Day A.D. 579, had baptized ten thousand Saxons. The monastery took the name of Minster, like that which was founded at the same time by her niece Domneva in the neighbouring isle of Thanet. She there ruled a community of seventy-seven nuns, until she learned that her sister Etheldreda, having fled from her husband, King Egfrid of Northumbria, according to the advice of S. Wilfred, had taken refuge in the marshes of their native country, and had there formed on the alder grown islet of Ely an asylum for souls resolute to serve God in solitude and virginity.

Sexburga then resolved to return to her own country, and become a simple nun under the crosier of her sister. "Farewell, my daughter," she said to her companions, who were gathered round her, "I leave you Jesus for your protector, His holy angels for companions, and one of my daughters for your superior . . . . . I go to East Anglia where I was born, in order to have my glorious sister Etheldreda for my mistress, and to take part immediately in her labours here below, that I may share her recompense above."

She was received with enthusiasm at Ely; the whole

community came forth to welcome her, and the two sister-queens wept for joy when they met. They lived together afterwards in the most tender union, rivalling each other in zeal for the service of God and the salvation of souls, Sexburga compelling herself always to take lessons of humility and fervour from her sister. Upon the death of Etheldreda, Sexburga re-placed her as abbess, and ruled the great East Anglian monastery for twenty years before she too found her rest near the tomb which she had erected to her sister.

[July 15

S. SWITHUN, B. OF WINCHESTER.
(A.D. 862.)

[Roman Martyrology, and York Kalendar of 1418. Sarum Kalendar of 1521, the Translation on July 15th, so also Reformed Anglican Kalendar. Authorities :—A metrical life by Wolstan, monk of Winchester (cca. 990), and a life by Gotselin the monk (cca. 1110). A much altered edition of this life was published by Surius, and again by the Bollandists, but a MS. of the original text of Gotselin, written in the 12th cent., far superior to the printed text, is preserved in the Arundel Library in the British Museum. Also William of Malmesbury "Gesta Pontif."]

DURING the melancholy period of the Danish invasions, from the reign of Egbert to the time when King Alfred restored peace to the island, science and literature seem to have been banished from our land. The name of S. Swithun stands alone conspicuous amidst the general gloom.

He appears to have been a native of Wessex; he was born in the reign of Egbert, probably at, or very soon after, the commencement of the 9th century. He was placed at an early age in the monastery of Winchester, where he was distinguished by his humility, and his application to study. He was ordained priest by Bishop Helmestan, in, or soon after, the year 830.

S. Swithun's virtue attracted the attention of King Egbert, who held him in such great regard, that he chose him as his spiritual director; and his name, as "priest of King Egbert," is found in a charter, which Witlaf, king of the Mercians, granted to the abbey of Croyland, in Lincolnshire. His reputation for learning was the cause of his being chosen instructor to Ethelwolf (or, as he was then more popularly called, Æthulf), son of Egbert. After a course of instruction, the young prince was ordained sub-deacon, and made his profession as a monk in Winchester. But on the death of his father, as he was the only son, and the royal line of the West Saxons would otherwise have failed, he obtained a dispensation from the pope, and married Osburga, the daughter of the noble cup-bearer, Oslac.

Egbert died in 836, and his son Ethelwolf was chosen king of the West Saxons. Bishop Helmestan died about the same time, and one of the first acts of Ethelwolf's reign was to accede to the petition of the monks of Winchester, and confer the vacant see on his friend and preceptor, Swithun.

S. Swithun was consecrated by Cealnoth, archbishop of Canterbury, to whom he made a profession of his faith, and vowed canonical obedience. He devoted himself

wholly to feed the flock of God committed to him; and
spent much of his time in spiritual exercises, and in the
care of the poor.

In 855, a synod of the clergy and nobles met at Winchester, at which the tributary princes of Mercia and East
Anglia were also present. King Ethelwolf bestowed on
the Church a tenth part of the produce of all the lands of
his kingdom, "for the honour of our Lord Jesus Christ, the
Blessed Virgin, and all Saints." He confirmed this gift by
a formal charter, which he afterwards solemnly laid on the
altar of the blessed Apostles at Rome. The church lands
were exempted at the same time from all secular services,
exactions, and tribute. The king also confirmed the
pension of Romescot, or Peter's pence, which had been
first offered to the see of Rome by Ina, king of the West
Saxons, in 726, and in 794 by Offa, king of the Mercians,
as a tribute of gratitude for the many signal favours which
England had received from the successors of S. Peter.

Ethelwolf was a remarkable example of a weak monarch,
who loved peace and retirement, placed suddenly upon a
throne in unusually difficult times. But his kingdom was
governed with skill, by the counsels of S. Swithun of
Winchester, and Bishop Alstane of Sherborne. The latter
was a statesman and a soldier, and led the king's armies in
person in many battles against the Danish invaders.

S. Swithun appears to have been chosen companion to
the king in his more private hours, and he exerted his
interest on all occasions in favour of the Church. After
the great battle of Akley,[1] 851, had checked the incursions
of the Danes for a season, S. Swithun persuaded the king
to renew the intercourse with the see of Rome, which had
been interrupted by so many years of trouble. Accordingly, in 853, Ethelwolf sent his youngest and favourite son

[1] Oak-lea in Surrey.

Alfred, then five years old, to Rome, with a large retinue of people of all ranks; and there are grounds for supposing that the royal child was conducted to the apostolic city by S Swithun himself.

Two years afterwards (in 855), Ethelwolf visited Rome in person, taking with him his son Alfred. He carried with him the tribute of the English people to the pope, as already mentioned, and presented him with a massive crown of gold. He also rebuilt the English school and hospital at Rome which had been founded by Ina, but which had been burned down.

On his way through France he married Judith, the daughter of Charles the Bald. This foreign match seems to have been distasteful to the Anglo-Saxon nobles; and when Ethelwolf arrived in England, he found a considerable portion of his subjects in arms against him, led by Bishop Alstane, and his own son Ethelbald.[1]

Ethelwolf avoided a civil war, by quietly yielding a large part of his kingdom to his son; and he only survived the partition two years and a half, dying in January, 858.

The influence of S. Swithun appears not to have ended with the death of Ethelwolf. Ethelbald married his stepmother, Judith, as had been done before by Eadbald, king of Kent. Such a marriage seems to have been allowed by old Saxon and German heathen custom; but as it was held to be unlawful among Christians, S. Swithun expostulated with the king, and it is said, that he succeeded in prevailing on him to submit to a separation. Judith after his death returned to her father's court, and afterwards married Baldwin, count of Flanders.

S. Swithun was a great benefactor to his own diocese, and to the city of Winchester. Besides building and repairing many churches, he erected the eastern bridge of

---

[1] So in Asser, but not in the Anglo-Saxon Chronicle.

Winchester with strong arches of stone. But he lived to see the city plundered, and in great part ruined, by the Danes, in 860.

S. Swithun was taken to his rest on the 2nd of July, 862, and by his own directions was buried in the churchyard. The situation of his grave was afterwards forgotten, till it was discovered in the 10th cent., in the time of Bishop Ethelwold, and in 971 the bones were translated into the cathedral church.   In 1079, Walkelyn, bishop of Winchester, laid the foundation of the present church, and in 1093 the relics of S. Swithun were removed into it.

There is a popular notion, that if it rain on S. Swithun's day (the feast of the translation, July 15th), it will continue to do so for six weeks.   None of the stories which are told in explanation are satisfactory; and they seem only to prove the total ignorance which prevails regarding it.

The bones of S. Swithun lie under a broad stone east of the choir in the presbytery.

S. WERBURGA, V. ABSS.

(BEGINNING OF 8TH CENTURY.)

[English Martyrology. Authorities :—Life of Goscelin, the monk (fl 1100), and mention in Bede, John of Brompton, Florence of Worcester, Hyden, Langherne, Simeon of Durham.]

WERBURGA, patroness of Chester, was born at Stone, in Staffordshire, and was the daughter of Wulfhere, King of Mercia, or the Midland English. From the lips of her sainted mother, Ermingilde, she received those first lessons of Christian truth which afterwards produced such beautiful fruit in her life.

Being one of four children, all trained under the same godly discipline, she is said to have excelled them all in virtue and discretion. Her mind was open to receive good impressions, and she listened with earnest attention to every word of instruction and advice. Thus, she " daily grew in grace, and in the knowledge of our Lord and Saviour Jesus Christ :" her mind continually expanding under the influence of holy thoughts and pure desires. At an age when most persons of her exalted position would have been found joining in the giddy whirl of pleasure, she found truest joy in contemplation of heavenly things, and holiest bliss, arising from a pure conscience chastened by fasting and sanctified by prayer. She daily assisted her mother in the performance of the whole Church Offices, and spent much time on her knees in the exercise of private devotions.

Having early resolved to devote herself to a life of virginal purity, she sought every opportunity to prepare her mind

for that holy state.   But she was not to overcome the world
without a struggle.   Temptations began to gather around
her.   The beauty of her person attracted a crowd of
admirers, who eagerly sought her hand in marriage.
Foremost among these was a prince of the West Saxons,
who offered her rich gifts and made flattering proposals.
She refused to accept his gifts; and to his proposals
answered that she had resolved to become the bride of
Christ, and wished no earthly spouse.

Another, and more violent temptation soon presented
itself.   Werbode, a powerful knight of her father's court,
backed by the influence of her father, entreated Werburga
to become his wife ; but to his entreaties she turned a deaf
ear.   Imagining that to this refusal she was influenced by
her two brothers, who were then under the instruction of
S. Chad, and resolving by fair or foul means to compass his
designs, Werbode sought an opportunity to murder the two
brothers, and thus remove them from his path.   In the
accomplishment of this diabolical design, he was, to a
certain extent, assisted by the father, whom he had in-
censed against his sons.   Werbode soon after died a
miserable death.   The king, stung by remorse, saw re-
flected, as in a mirror, all the deeds of his past life, and
remembered how he had promised to extirpate idolatry from
his dominions, but had failed to perform his vow.   With
earnestness he began to atone for his faults ; destroyed the
idols and converted their temples into churches, built the
great abbey of Peterborough, founded the priory of Stone,
and in every way endeavoured to propagate the true faith
among his people.

Seeing this happy change in his disposition, Werburga
revealed to her father the earnest desire of her heart, and
earnestly entreated his permission to consecrate herself
wholly to God.   At first he appeared to be very grieved,

S. WERBURGA. From Cahier.

but yielding at length to her passionate entreaties, Wulfhere, attended by his whole court, conducted her with great state to the convent of Ely. Here they were met at the gates by a long procession of nuns, singing hymns of praise and thanksgiving to God. Werburga, falling on her knees, begged of the royal abbess, S. Etheldreda, that she might be received as a postulant. Having obtained her request, the voice of praise again ascended to heaven, the virgins chanting the *Te Deum*, as they returned to the convent. Now followed the usual trials; Werburga was first stripped of her costly apparel, her rich coronet was exchanged for a poor veil, purple and silks and gold were replaced by a rough coarse habit, and she resigned herself into the hands of her superior, henceforward to live only to Christ.

The virgin, with great fervour, now devoted herself to God. Her affections being weaned from earthly things, were fixed more firmly upon those things which are above. By prayer and fasting, by self-sacrifice and mortification, by obedience and penance, she sought to sanctify her soul and body, that she might present them, a holy and acceptable sacrifice, unto God.

After many years she was chosen, at the request of her uncle King Ethelred, to superintend all the religious houses for women in his kingdom. When she entered upon this larger sphere of duty, she laboured with earnest diligence to make all the houses under her care models of exact monastic discipline. Through the liberality of her uncle, she was enabled to found new convents at Trentham, in Gloucestershire; Hanbury, in Staffordshire; and Weedon, in Northamptonshire. These remained for several centuries as evidences of her godly zeal. The king also, at her request, founded the collegiate church of S. John the Baptist, in the suburbs of West Chester, and gave to S. Egwin the ground for the great abbey of Evesham.

S. Werburga, both by precept and example, sought to develope the religious life in those committed to her charge, and many through her influence were won from a life of dissipation and vice to a life of holiness and love.

God, in answer to continual prayers, had crowned her with many spiritual and celestial blessings. The old chroniclers say that she became the most perfect pattern of meekness, humility, patience, and purity. Her fastings and mortifications were almost incredible. She never took more than one meal during the day, and that of the coarsest food: seeking in this to emulate the lives of those fathers of the desert who shed such radiance over the Eastern and African Church. Beside the usual monastic offices, she was in the habit of reciting, upon her knees, the whole of the Psalter daily. She often remained in the church all night, bathed in tears and prostrate in prayer.

In the exercise of these holy devotions she lived to a ripe old age. Receiving at last some premonitions of her approaching departure, she made a farewell visit to all the houses under her care, and exhorted the inmates to prepare for the coming of the heavenly Bridegroom. Then retiring to the convent at Trentham, she quietly waited her departure. The messenger soon came, and found the bride ready, and so with quiet faith and perfect trust she went to the home of her Spouse, on the 3rd of February, 699.

Her corpse, in accordance with her own directions, was conveyed to the monastery at Hanbury. It was interred with great honour, and there remained until the year 708. Then it was disinterred in presence of King Ceolred and many bishops, and transferred to a costly shrine. The old chroniclers say that it was found incorrupt, and remained so until A.D. 875, when, for fear of the Danes, who were invading the country, the shrine was carried to Chester. The body, however, fell to dust soon after its translation. In course of time a stately church was erected over the relics; this became the cathedral, and as such exists to this day.

During the reign of Henry VIII., the shrine was desecrated, and the holy relics of S. Werburga scattered abroad. What remained of the costly shrine was afterwards converted into an episcopal throne, and may still be seen, carved with the curious images of kings of Mercia, ancestors of S. Werburga, who flourished eleven centuries ago. To this day it is used as the throne of the bishops of Chester.

March 17.]

S. WITHBURGA, V.

(A.D. 743.)

[Some ancient martyrologies, others on July 8th. Authority:—The Ely Chronicle, and a Life supposed to be by Goscelin, the historian of S. Werburga.]

THE royal race of the Uffings of East Anglia was remarkable for the crowd of saints which it produced. King Anna, who married the sister of Hilda, the celebrated abbess of Whitby, became father of three daughters and a son. The son became in his turn the father of three daughters, two of whom were in succession abbesses of Hackness in Northumbria, founded by their grand-aunt S. Hilda, and the last, Eadburga, became abbess of Repton.

The three daughters of Anna,—Etheldreda, Sexburga, and Withburga—are all counted among the saints. Withburga was sent into the country to be nursed, and remained there till she heard, while still quite young, of her father's death on the battle-field. She resolved immediately to seek a refuge for the rest of her life in claustral virginity. She chose as her asylum a modest remnant of her father's lands at East Dereham, in Norfolk, and there built a little monastery. But she was so poor that she, her companions, and the masons who built her future dwelling, had to live on dry bread alone. One day, after she had prayed long to the blessed Virgin, she saw two does come out of the neighbouring forest to drink at a stream whose pure current watered the secluded spot. Their udders were heavy with milk, and they permitted themselves to be milked by the virginal hands of Withburga's companions, returning every day to the same place, and thus furnishing a sufficient supply for the nourishment of the little community and its workmen. This lasted till the ranger of the royal domains, a savage and wicked man, who regarded with an evil eye the rising house of God, undertook to hunt down the two helpful animals. He pursued them with his dogs across the country, but, in attempting to leap a high hedge, his horse was impaled on a post, and the hunter broke his neck.

Withburga ended her life in this poor and humble solitude ; but the fragrance of her gentle virtues spread far and wide. The fame of her holiness went through all the surrounding country. The veneration given to her by the people of Norfolk was maintained with the pertinacity common to the Anglo-Saxon race, and went so far that, two centuries after her death, they armed themselves to defend her relics from the monks of Ely, who came, by the king's command, to unite them to those of her sisters at Ely.

There still exists at East Dereham a well bearing the name of S. Withburga. It is fed by a spring rising in the very place where the saint's body was laid before its translation to Ely.

S. WULSTAN, B. OF WORCESTER.

(A.D. 1095.)

[Anglican and German and Roman Martyrologies. Authorities: his life by Florence of Worcester (D. 1118),[1] and William of Malmesbury, written 47 years after the death of S. Wulstan; another in Roger of Wendover, and numerous notices in other old English historians. He is called variously Wulstan and Wulfstan.]

S. WULSTAN was born in Warwickshire of pious parents. His father's name was Ealstan, and his mother's Wulfgeova. Both his parents were so devoted to the religious life, that, by mutual consent, they retired into monastic houses. Inspired by such examples, but chiefly by his mother's persuasion, Wulfstan quitted the world whilst yet young, and took the monastic habit in the same monastery in Worcester where his father had devoted himself to the service of God. He was there ordained deacon, and then priest, by the bishop. Observing a very strict course of life, he soon became remarkable for his vigils, fasting and prayers. In consequence of his discipline of himself, he was first appointed master of the novices, and afterwards, on account of his acquaintance with the ecclesiastical services, precentor and treasurer of the church. Being now intrusted with the custody of the church, he embraced the opportunities it afforded him for being almost perpetually in the sacred edifice, spending whole nights before the altar in prayer; and when he was exhausted with fatigue, he lay on one of the church benches, and placed his prayer-book beneath his head as a pillow.

After some time, on the death of the prior, Bishop Aldred appointed Wulstan to succeed him. As prior, he preached every Lord's Day to the people, with so great unction, that they were moved to tears. One of the monks grumbled, and

---

[1] Florence knew S. Wulstan personally, as appears from his account of his vigils. He says, "He sometimes went four days and nights without sleep,—a thing we could hardly have believed, if we had not heard it from his own mouth."

said that Wulfstan forgot his place,—it was the office of the bishop to preach, and that of the monk to hold his tongue. Hearing this, Wulfstan said, " My brother, the Word of God is not bound."

Although very abstemious and moderate in his diet, he had not refrained from meat, till one day that roast goose was being prepared for dinner, the fragance filled the church, and Wulstan, who was at the altar celebrating mass, was so distracted with the delicious odour, for he was very hungry, as it was the late choral mass, that he could not collect his thoughts. Then, filled with shame, before he left the altar he vowed never to touch meat again, and he kept this vow to his dying day.

On the elevation of Aldred, Bishop of Worcester, to the archbishopric of York, by unanimous consent of the clergy and laity in the election of a successor, Wulstan was chosen; the king having granted them permission to elect whom they pleased.

It chanced that the legates from the Pope were present at the election, but neither they nor the clergy and people could persuade Wulstan to accept the charge, of which he declared himself to be unworthy. At last, being sharply re-proved for his obstinate wilfulness by Wulfsi, a hermit, and being strongly urged by S. Edward the Confessor, then king, he yielded, and was consecrated on the Feast of the Nativity of the Blessed Virgin Mary, 1062.

As bishop, Wulstan maintained the same severity towards himself; every day he sang the late high mass ; it being usual for the priests to take the choral mass by weeks, in turns, it being very trying, as the celebrant had to remain fasting till a late hour. Wulstan not only sang the high mass daily, but also all the canonical hours, and when he rode on journeys, he had his book open before him on the pommel of his saddle, and he chanted aloud the psalms of David.

As the old church and monastic buildings reared by S. Oswald were being demolished, to make way for more splendid edifices, Wulstan stood one day, and looked at the roofless church, and the walls that were being torn down, and his eyes filled with tears. "Why should you weep," said a monk, standing by; "you should rather laugh, to see the meanness of the first house swept away, to make room for a glorious second one." "No," answered Wulstan, "I see nothing to rejoice over in the demolition of the work of our Saints. True, they knew not how to rear a stately building; but under a mean roof, they offered the adorable sacrifice to God with great devotion, and set saintly examples to their flock; and we—we collect and carve the stones of the material temple, and neglect the edification of that which is spiritual—the souls of men."

Below him in church sat a curly-headed choir boy. One day the bishop bent down, and laying his hand on the glossy curls, said, "All these will fall off one day!" Then the boy in alarm, turned round and said, "Oh, save my curls for me!" "My child, do not fear, as long as I live you shall retain your abundant hair." And so he did, for many long years, till Wulstan died, and then, says the chronicler who records this strange little incident, his hair came off as the bishop had foretold.[1]

When William the Conqueror established himself in England, he not only gave the lands to his Norman nobles, but also the bishoprics to his Norman clergy. "Wulstan is a fool, he cannot speak French!" said William, and he ordered Lanfranc, his Norman Archbishop of Canterbury, to depose the plain Saxon Bishop of Worcester, on the

---

[1] S. Wulstan sometimes joked; but the specimen recorded by Malmesbury is not striking for wit, nor for its reverence, wherefore I give it in Latin. Being asked why he wore lamb's wool garments in winter, instead of cat's skin like the other clergy he answered, "Nunquam audivi cantari Cattus Dei, sed Agnus Dei; ideo non catto, sed agno volo calefieri."

charge of ignorance. A conclave was held in Westminster Abbey in 1074, to decide a dispute between Robert, Archbishop of York, and Lanfranc, Archbishop of Canterbury, as to the question whether the diocese of Worcester belonged to the northern or the southern province, and at the same time to deprive Wulstan. When called in question as to his slender attainments in learning, he rose and said, "We have not sung Sext yet. Let us chant the office first, and I will answer afterwards."

But those around him remonstrated, saying, "Let us do our business first, and we can sing the service afterwards; we shall become objects of ridicule to the king and nobles, if we keep them waiting till we have done our office."

"No!" exclaimed Wulstan; "the duty to God must be done first, and then we will consider the petty disputes of men." Having sung the service, he directly proceeded to the council chamber. To his dependants, who were desirous of withholding him, and who could not be persuaded that their cause was not in danger, he said, "Know for certain, that I here see the holy archbishops, Dunstan of Canterbury and Oswald of York, defending me this day by their prayers, and they will darken the understandings of my gainsayers." Then he gave his benediction to a monk who could speak Norman French, but imperfectly at best, and ordered him to state his case for him.[1]

There stood the grave long-bearded Saxon bishop arraigned for ignorance before the Norman king, and his smooth-shaven[2] Norman prelates. Wulstan, the representative of the people, Lanfranc of the nobles; Wulstan, the bishop of the conquered, and Lanfranc of the conquerors. When the poor Saxon peasants had come to him

---

[1] So far William of Malmesbury, who abruptly closes, saying that he will no longer torture the patience of his readers. What follows is from Roger of Wendover.

[2] Dr. Rock: Church of our Fathers, II. p. 99, plate.

at Worcester, and had complained that these Norman invaders trampled down their corn, and robbed them of their cattle, and ground them down with taxes; "They are God's scourge, these Normans, punishing us for our sins, my children," said Wulstan. And now he was to be deprived of his office by these invaders, that a Norman might occupy his stool, and shepherd with his crook the Saxon bondsmen. The council decided, in accordance with the royal pleasure, that Wulstan was too ignorant to deserve to retain his see, and that therefore he must resign his pastoral staff and ring. The ring, the token that he was wedded to his diocese before God, that he said he would never resign, in life or in death. "I received this ring without coveting it, and I will bear it with me to my grave."[1] But the staff, the token of jurisdiction, that he could be deprived of, so rising from his place, with unruffled composure, and placid countenance, holding his staff, he said, "Truly, my Lord Archbishop, truly I know that I am unworthy of this honour, nor fit to bear this burden, nor sufficient to endure the labour. I knew this when the clergy elected me, and when the bishops urged me, and when my own master, King Edward, invited me. He, with the authority of the apostolic see, laid this burden on my shoulders, and ordered me to be invested with the episcopate, by the token of this staff. Now thou desirest of me this pastoral staff, which thou gavest me not; thou demandest of me the surrender of the office thou laidest not on me. I, indeed, am well aware of my ignorance, and yielding to the sentence of this holy conclave, I resign my staff—not to thee, but to him who gave it me." Saying this he went forth from the chapter house to the tomb of S. Edward the Confessor, and standing before the stone, he cried, "Thou knowest, O my Master! how reluctantly I received this

[1] Roger of Wendover, and Capgrave.

burden, how often I fled away from it; how, when sought, that it might be imposed on me, I secreted myself. I confess that I am a fool, but thou didst constrain me. There lacked not the election of the brethren, the entreaty of the people, the will of the bishops, the favour of the nobles; but none of these things weighed with me like thy authority; it was thy will that bent mine. And now we have a new king, a new law, a new archbishop, who found new rights and declare new sentences. They convince thee of error, who commanded, and me of presumption, who obeyed. Therefore, not to them who demand, but to thee who gavest; not to them, fallible, walking in darkness, but to thee who hast been led forth into the clear light of very truth, and hast escaped out of this region of error and ignorance, to thee I resign my staff, to thee I surrender the cure of those thou didst commend to me, to thee I commit them in confidence, knowing well thy merits."

Having said this, he slowly raised his hand a little, and said. "My lord and king, accept this, and surrender it to whom thou choosest!" Then he struck the staff into the sepulchral stone, and laying aside his pontifical habit, he seated himself, as a monk, among the monks.

Was there ever a grander incident in English Church history? Was there ever a nobler speech uttered by an English bishop?

Then all, surprised, saw that the staff stood in the stone; and one ran and told Lanfranc, but he believed it not, and bade Gundulf, Bishop of Rochester, to whom he had promised the bishopric of Worcester, to go and bring back the staff. So Gundulf went, but the staff was immovably imbedded in the stone.

Then the archbishop and the king went to the tomb, and sought to wrench the staff from where it stood, but they were unable. Lanfranc at once turned, and coming straight down to where the monk sat, he bowed to him, and said, "Verily God resisteth the proud and giveth grace unto the humble. Thy simplicity was scorned by us, brother, but thy righteousness is made clear as the light. Our wisdom has been brought to naught, and thy ignorance has prevailed. Take then again that charge which we unadvisedly deprived thee of, but which we, by our authority and the judgment of God, commit to thee once more."

But Wulstan hesitated; however, being urged vehemently by those who stood by, he went to the tomb again, and said:—"Now, my lord and king, to whose judgment I commended myself, and to whom I resigned my staff, show me what is thy pleasure. Thou hast preserved thine honour, thou hast made manifest my innocence. If thine old sentence stands, restore to me my staff; if not, yield it to whom thou wilt!" Then he put forth his hand, and touched the staff, and he removed it at once with ease.[1]

To Lanfranc and Wulstan, acting conjointly, is due the cessation of the slave traffic in England. It was the custom of the English to sell slaves to the Irish, and this was subject to a tax which passed into the royal exchequer. "The credit of this action," says Malmesbury, [2] "I know not whether to attribute to Lanfranc, or to Wulstan, who would scarcely have induced the king, reluctant from the profit it produced to him, to this measure, had not Lanfranc commended it, and Wulstan, powerful through the sanctity of his character, commended it by episcopal authority."

Having taken the oath of allegiance to William, Wulstan remained faithful. When, in the same year, 1074, some of the Saxon earls rose against the Conqueror, Wulstan and

[1] This most striking incident is not mentioned by Florence of Worcester, or William of Malmesbury, but occurs in Roger of Wendover and Matthew of Westminster.

[2] Chronicle, lib. III.

the abbot of Evesham, supported by the sheriff of Worcester and Walter de Lacy, prevented their junction, by raising their vassals and occupying the ford of the Severn.[1]

In the Barons' revolt, 1088, " Bernard du Neuf-Marché, Roger de Lacy, who had lately wrested Hereford from the king, and Ralph de Mortimer, with the vassals of the Earl of Shrewsbury, having assembled a numerous army of English, Normans and Welsh, burst into the province of Worcester, declaring that they would burn the city of Worcester, plunder the Church of God and S. Mary, and take summary vengeance on the inhabitants for their loyalty to the king. On hearing this, the reverend father Wulstan, Bishop of Worcester, a man of deep piety and dove-like simplicity, beloved alike by God and the people he governed, faithful to the king as his earthly lord, was in great tribulation; but soon rallying, by God's mercy, prepared to stand manfully by his people and city. While they armed themselves to repel the enemy, he poured forth supplications in the impending danger, exhorting his people not to despair. Meanwhile, the Normans, taking counsel, entreated the bishop to remove from the church into the castle, saying that his presence there would give them more security, if they were in great peril, for they loved him much. Such was his extraordinary kindness of heart, that from duty to the king, and regard for them, he assented to their request.

" Thereupon, the bishop's retainers made ready, and the garrison and the whole body of citizens assembled, declaring that they would encounter the enemy on the other side of the Severn, if the bishop would give them leave. Taking their arms, and being arrayed for battle, they met the bishop, as he was going to the castle, and besought him to grant their desire, to which he freely assented. 'Go,' said

[1] Florence of Worcester.

he, 'My sons, go in peace, go in confidence, with God's blessing and mine. Trusting in God, I promise you that no sword shall hurt you this day. Be loyal, and do valiantly for the safety of the people and the city.'" The victory was complete. The rebels were routed, and the king's liege-men and the bishop's retainers returned home in triumph, without the loss of a single man.[1]

He died in the year 1095, on January the 19th, and was buried with his ring on his finger. "God suffered no man to remove from his finger the ring with which he had received episcopal consecration," says Florence of Worcester; "that the holy man might not appear to forfeit his engagement to his people, to whom he had often protested that he would not part with it during his life, nor even on the day of his burial."

[1] Florence of Worcester.

S. WULSTAN, BISHOP OF WORCESTER.
From a Design by A. Welby Pugin.

Also published by
Llanerch:

LIVES OF THE
BRITISH SAINTS
by
Baring-Gould and Fisher

LIVES OF THE
NORTHUMBRIAN SAINTS
by
S. Baring-Gould

LIVES OF THE
SCOTTISH SAINTS
by
W. Metcalfe

NORTHUMBRIAN CROSSES
by
W. G. Collingwood

SYMBOLISM OF THE
CELTIC CROSS
by
Derek Bryce

From booksellers.
For a complete list, '
write to: '
Llanerch Enterprises,
Felinfach, Lampeter,
Dyfed, Wales,
SA48 8PJ.